p9 an chooniroble dream

16, 21
22
30 - Bagh Nux has S

Did you try suicide?

48

53

62

80

p 177 od

p24 "to the world"

p44 child psychology
47 Close the door
p73 - him not he
p75 - seem not seems
p78 - extra comma

The Rocky Hill

89 - sixth (no's)

p 12 stupedous? — is this quite the right word?
145-6 looked at the moon.
p166 where
p171 a trace
146 needs question mark
p198 erupts

The Rocky Hill

Stories And Poems

Ilana Haley

To order additional copies of this book, contact:
Xlibris Corporation
1-888-795-4274
www.Xlibris.com
Orders@Xlibris.com
67187

DEDICATION

This book is dedicated to my beloved father and mother.

All the stories in this book are based on real events, but all characters are the fruit of the writer's imagination.

I want to thank all the friends who helped me to finally publish this book, especially to Oded Wolkstein for his wonderful editing and encouragement, and to Augi Augenstein and Bruria Bat-Zvi for designing the cover. I also would like to give thanks to Lorie Adams from Xlibris Publication, for her patience, help, and being so sweet.

But specially I thank you, all my readers. I hope with all my heart that you enjoy reading this book.

A few words from the editor:

Every story and poem of Ilana's is a journey into an emotional transformation, black holes in the cosmology of the soul. These are special kinds of stories and poetry. She writes from the depth of pain that is never forgotten. Under the warm voice flows another voice: knowing, thinking, and harsh. These stories and poems may be read as a string of separations. But the aloneness of Ilana is wonder. In her aloneness, Ilana finds, one after another, the moments of love that were captured in her glass of words—words that are the wound, the bandage, and forever the salt that awakens the pain which never gets old. Ilana embroiders the pain of her characters in words; she is faithful to tell it pure and direct.

Oded Wolkstein, editor.

CONTENTS

5. DESERT DANCE *(LIAT)*

6. THE ROSES ARE DYING *(MAYA)*

7. GIVE US A KISS

THE ROCKY HILL

(RITA)

I brought you the flowers you loved so much, and I hear you say, "Michal'e, Flowers should stay where they belong, in the ground." And you had filled every empty spot in the house with potted plants and growing flowers and said, "If I truly, truly wanted to, I could speak to the roots and watch the flowers grow." And when Father said, "Don't put crazy ideas into the child's head," you ignored him. But you see, I remembered about the flowers, and I dug them out with the roots,—so I can plant them here where the ground is fresh and damp, like after the rain, which you had loved so much.

Remember when life seemed like a forever dream? And it was all right to leave the children at home alone, and people didn't lock the doors because the kibbutz was a safe place, or so everyone thought, and every day we played in the fields, and the mornings were always blue and the birds screamed in the trees, and fragrance of wildflowers wafted in the air, and millions of snails and earthworms appeared after the rain. And a honey sun smiled at us, painting with gold our hair and eyes and face, sprinkling our noses with big brown spots.

And then the wars started, and all of us boys wanted to be paratroopers, and in class, we read the Bible every day because we were told it was our heritage and history. And Old Gara was still alive, and Sam the Cat was slinking around, and Father's hair was still brown and his tanned face taut. And Nati was a mischievous tiny girl who at age seven, I was crazy about.

But not to tell you this, I have run away from the army camp and came here all messed up and sweating and without breath. I came to tell you finally about that night when a storm rampaged outside, and I was so scared, and you weren't there. I still have nightmares about that night, and that crazy Memorial Day keeps haunting me like a demon from Dante's Hell, and I want to tell you how it was then when I was only a little boy. Maybe, only maybe, it will ease the pain.

Wherever you are, Mother, listen well. This time listen really well.

Once when I was about seven, I was lying on my stomach on the floor of my room, trying to concentrate on a jigsaw puzzle, waiting for Nati to come play with me; but outside the wind roared, and the windows shook, and I heard sounds like moans around the house, and I knew that Nati would never make it in that storm.

But in spite of my anxiety, I smiled because I never knew what Nati was up to; she was mischievous and daring and loved adventures,—never afraid of anything. Maybe a little of her mother because sometimes, in the midst of a game, she would suddenly say, "I have to go now, my mother is waiting," and I would notice her face becoming suddenly tense and her lips trembled. You adored Nati; you would hug her and kiss her and say, "Natushka, you are so pretty." And then you would sigh and say, "I always wanted a girl," and I was jealous.

But you never loved anyone like you love Big Micha, even after he left you and joined the dead. I could never understand why you waste so much love on a dead man. After you weren't with us anymore, Father hardly ever spoke, and his hair turned white, and his face cracked, and his eyes—it's difficult for me to describe his eyes because suddenly there was nothing in his eyes. So, if eyes can be empty, Father's eyes were empty after what you did. Most of the time, he wandered like a spirit in the olive grove or sat near the window with the view of the lawn, the acacia tree, the daisies, and the daffodils; and when I spoke to him, he would look at me and say, confused, "What, what did you say, child?" At such moments, I could have killed you myself.

Sometimes Nati would come and, for a few moments, relieve Father from the depression, with her stories about the field, the sheep, and the jokes of her grandfather, Ezra, whom she loved even more than she had loved her grandmother, Marta, who died of cancer. After her grandmother died, Nati said that it is all right because her grandmother is now in a place full of light, and rain falls there all the time. Her grandmother was crazy about rain; she said rain is the essence of life.

The thought that Nati wouldn't come because of the storm made me stand up abruptly and upset the puzzle, and I looked at the mess of little cardboard pieces and snorted in disgust and screwed up my eyes and bared my teeth and screamed, "I'm a tiger! I'm a man-eating beast!" I roared, running around the room with claws ready to gouge the enemy's eyes. Then I was Sam the Cat, and I crouched on the floor and arched my back, feeling the hair bristle on my neck, and didn't make a sound. My whole body tensed, ready for war. But the moment I sprang into the air ready to catch my prey, I began to wheeze and choke and collapsed on the floor. Again, I was only a little boy with asthma—a questionable fun, especially when you are all alone in a house you suddenly distrust.

I turned on the radio hoping music would distract me—even the news, anything. But the radio roared and whistled as if a whole pack of hounds and hyenas were caught inside it, so I turned it off and ran to the window, and I watched how the wind teased the clouds, and the whole world was charged with electricity as furious lightning struck a messy sky, followed by stupendous booms and distant rumbles, and I couldn't shut the shutters that were banging against the wall of the house, and as the wind intensified, I was certain the house swayed. I looked at the clock, it was only a little past six, and you were still out because it was your turn to work in the Dining Hall. And I imagined you standing behind the counter handing out dishes, and I could smell the peas and the roast potatoes and the chicken, and I saw your face shining with sweat and your hands slippery with grease and your green eyes dull and gray and full of fatigue.

I knew how much you loathed working in the Dining Hall, because the first thing you did when you came home was to kick off your shoes and rub your toes and complain that your legs were swollen and your feet were sore, and that you smelled of garlic and rancid oil. "Disgusting," I remember you say once, your face contorted with distaste. And Father looked at you and said with a special smile he kept only for you, "You're so spoiled, Rita." You stared at him, and I saw your eyes narrow. "Wise guy," you said, your voice scratchy. And Father said, "I didn't mean to upset you." And when he brought you a cup of coffee, you pushed away his hand. "Be careful," he said, and the smile was gone from his face. You said you were sorry, and I stuck my fingers deep into my ears from dread that you'd fight again. "Michal'e," you said, "take your fingers out of your ears. It isn't healthy," and you asked, "did you water the plants?" and

I muttered aha, and you smiled at me, and I saw a net of tiny wrinkles around your eyes.

But worst of all were the nights when you were too exhausted to sit on my bed and sing to me because, when you sang to me, your small soft voice made me feel so . . . But here I always reached the boundary of my thoughts because, at the age of seven, I didn't have words to articulate my feelings when you sang to me.

Father was at a secretariat meeting where he spent most of his time, arguing with Old Gara about winter crops and the critical (I didn't know then what critical meant) water problem, and whether they should keep or get rid of the olive grove, or how many new members could the kibbutz ~~can~~ absorb this year.

And that horrible night when I felt as if there was no one, nothing in the entire world except the storm, the thought of you and Father set off a memory as distinct as the sound of the thunder that shook the windows, a memory of an early summer evening when I was playing with my tanks and soldiers in a corner of the living room. At that particular evening, you and Father had returned from the Dining Hall a little later than usual, and Father settled at his usual place, at a small table under the window with the view of the lawn and the acacia tree and the daisies and the daffodils and opened the newspaper. You placed on the table a plate full of freshly baked cookies, which filled the room with aroma of vanilla, pecans, and raisins. "Enjoy, Eli," you said. And then you came over to me and cupped my chin and lifted my face to yours and kissed me on my lips and gave me two cookies, and I swallowed them hardly chewing. "Take it easy, Michal'e," you said, there are plenty," and you laughed and gave me another kiss. Then you stood by the little gas stove, waiting for the water to boil for coffee.

You looked so pretty, dressed in a white silk shirt and new blue jeans, your hair, loose, fell in waves and tangles all the way to your shoulders, and your eyes sparkled green and deep. I couldn't take my eyes off you. I prayed in my heart that you'd look at me, but you poured for Father a cup of coffee and asked, "How was your day, Eli?" Without lifting his eyes from the paper, Father said, "Like any other day, arguments, endless arguments." You laughed and said, "Is that so? It seems to me that all you ever do in those meetings is argue." Father didn't think it was funny. He said, "Yeah, so it seems," and he began tapping with his teaspoon on the cookie plate, a habit that drove you nuts until you said, and your voice was cutting, "Stop it, Eli." And he stopped. After that you and Father sat for a time and didn't speak at all, only drank the bitter coffee. You didn't laugh anymore.

I continued to play with my tanks and soldiers, imagining myself a general in the commando unit, my soldiers charging heroically, and my tanks perfectly lined up ready to attack, and corpses are strewn all over the battlefield, and the enemy almost defeated. "Fire! Fire!" I shouted and clapped my hands together, a habit keeping the palms of my hands always slightly red. Remember? And you said suddenly, and your voice was sharp as hail, "Michal'e, why do you always play war? Go play outside, it's healthier." And I was stunned by your sudden anger. I had been playing war for as long as I could remember myself. All the boys played war. And all I could think to say was, because, and you looked at me suspiciously and said, "Because why? Don't be a wise guy with me." And your outburst confused me so; I wanted to cry. And then Father lifted his eyes from the paper and said, "Boys play war, Rita." You didn't say anything and began to eat the cookies very fast, and didn't pay attention to the crumbs falling on the table and on the floor around your chair, and I was so surprised because I have never seen you eating like that. You were always so pedantic and neat—even compulsively so in my opinion.

Suddenly Father's voice thundered, "Listen, Rita!" You stopped eating and looked at him with startled eyes, and my eyelids began to twitch. And you said, "Don't yell, Eli, I'm not deaf." And my father said that important decisions should be made by the younger generation. Again, you told him not to yell and asked him what was he talking about, and he said that he was talking about the last secretariat meeting and how the old people had been driving him insane with their old ideas. I saw how the line between your eyebrows deepened, and you asked why. And Father said, "Leave it up to them and we'd be back to using mules and plows. I tell you, Rita, older people should know when it's time to quit and make room for younger people. You should hear the nostalgia in their voices when they talk about the *good old days,* when they still lived in tents and didn't have electricity or running water. You would think they had a feast then instead of swamps, malaria, and typhoid fever."

You were silent for a long time, gazing into space; then suddenly you said, in a voice that made me wish I could run to you and hug you, that their *good old days* sound so romantic, and that now our men die in wars and our children play war, "War, always war. Is it better to die in a war, Eli?" And the pitch of your voice was unusually high and tense, and your eyes were so sad. "I know, I know," Father said, "wars are terrible, but it's time for the kibbutz to change. The pioneering days are long over." Without looking at him, you said, "You have a stone for a heart, Eli," and you began talking about the days when you and Big Micha had spent many summer dawns in the olive grove, watching the sunlight play on the Judean hills. "Each time," you said, "the hills looked different. Sometimes clear and close, other times covered with clouds or fog, but"—and your voice became hushed and silky—"the real magic was at night when . . ." You didn't finish your sentence because Father roared, "Enough! This thing has got to stop!" And he stood up abruptly, shoving the chair in big anger. And you continued to talk about your nights in the olive grove with Big Micha as if you were alone in the world; then Father's elbow hit the cup, spilling the coffee, which spread in a big blotch on the tablecloth. "Damn it, Rita, shut up!" he shouted and, with shaking fingers, lit a cigarette. I heard him breathing hard. I thought in my heart that you weren't fair, even cruel, and I didn't want to think of you that way.

Father began wandering about the room; then stopped in front of your chair and said, "Big Micha, that's all you're able to think about. You haven't heard a word I've said. This thing has got to stop for the child's sake and mine." And you sat stiff and still, your eyes following the coffee stain spreading on the tablecloth until at last you looked at him and said, "You shouldn't have married me, Eli." I saw how Father's face suddenly turned ashen and so sad, and he said in a strange voice, "Rita, I love you." You lifted to him a drained face and said that you were so sorry for your outburst and that this had been a terrible day and you're so tired. And then you picked up the newspaper and glanced at the headlines and said, "Bad news, it's so terrible, all this bombing and killing and hate and—" But again you didn't finish your words because Father snatched the paper out of your hands, and lifted you from the chair, and pulled you to him, and pressed your body tightly to his. "Rita, Rita," he said, and his heavy face was buried in your hair. I didn't like it. You were so tiny and seemed so breakable, and he was so big and rough. It seemed to me that one of his hands could cover your whole body, and I was terrified that he might break you. And you said, "I'm sorry, Eli, so sorry," and by the shaking of your shoulders, I knew that you were weeping, your face pressed against his massive chest. And he caressed your hair and kept saying, "It's all right, it's all right," but his voice sounded like when you walk on gravel.

And while you and Father were carrying on, I sat in the corner of the room and trembled, and I felt the blood drumming in my temples and was dizzy and confused because I didn't understand anything from what I heard. I was sure that you had completely forgotten my presence in the room, and as always, when you behaved this way, my throat choked, and my chest tightened. I longed to see you laughing and happy and light but you were sad, always sad, or angry.

And when I no longer could bear the tension, I left my soldiers and tanks scattered on the floor and went outside and sat on the grass and threw stones at Sam the Cat. And there was the cat, and there I was, and for a while, we stood growling and hissing and baring our teeth, and then I heard you calling through the open window, "Michal'e, again you're abusing the cat? Let him be, it's time for bed. If you hurry, I'll read you a story." But I didn't move. "I don't want a story," I said, "I want you to sing to me," and I heard you sigh. "Not tonight," you said in a nervous voice, "I'm tired." And when still I didn't move, you said in this irritating voice, "My sweetheart." But I insisted that you sing to me and said, "Lie by me for only few minutes, Mama." And you pleaded; "Come in, Michal'e, now, please," and your eyes were green again.

That night, I won. You sat on my bed and read to me a sad story about a boy named David Copperfield and sang about raisins and almonds, about the moon and the fields, and then you lay down at my side and fell asleep while I stayed awake and watched over you. At that moment, we were only the two of us, alone. And I didn't know when I fell asleep and you returned to your room.

The next day, when I returned from school, I couldn't find my soldiers and tanks. They were not in their usual place in the wooden box under the bed, and I searched the entire house, but they disappeared. I didn't ask anything, only went to the bathroom, locked the door with the key, sat on the toilet, and cried.

And on that stormy night, when those thoughts sucked me in and you were not there, I imagined myself as a bird flying far, far away. And you? You're thinking of me and missing me and crying and pleading and calling me to come back to you.

Suddenly a terrible thought struck me—what if you forget me? Never again think of me? And I couldn't hold back and wet my pants like a baby. I ran to my room, and banged the door shut, and peeled off my pants, and washed my legs that stunk with urine, and changed into my pajamas, and kicked the evidence of my shame under the bed. And shivering, I hid under the blanket and covered my head with the pillow, desperately trying not to think and shutting off the boom of the thunder that became a distant rumble that turned into the loud, clear voice of my father saying to you what I often heard him say, "An accident, it's always an accident. What are we going to do about these accidents?" And you answered, "It will pass, it will pass. Give the child time." And Father said, "It is so embarrassing. He's already seven years old and in second grade. He should be sleeping in the Children House like the other children, but no, he has to sleep at home because he still wets his bed. What are we going to do with him?" And you said, "These things happen you know, and besides, I like it that he sleeps at home. If they'd ask my opinion, all the children should sleep at home." And Father said, "We've been discussing this matter in the meetings. Many parents want the children home at night. We've decided to bring this particular problem to a general vote next Saturday. Personally, I'm against it." And you said, "But, Eli, you're always talking about changes. Big changes." And my father answered, "Well, some things should not change, and this is one of them. The children's place is in the Children's House, together. It heightens their sense of communal spirit and toughens them up. But this entire aside for the moment, what do you intend to do about the child? What is the matter with him?" And you said, "I don't know, Eli, I just don't know." You thought for a moment then said, "We probably should take him to see a psychologist," and it sounded to me like some kind of a conspiracy. And there under my blanket, in the dark, I imagined you shaking your head and sighing, and I saw your face clearly, and my panic intensified, and I began to think that you'd never come home. So, I tossed back the blanket and sat up shaking, and snatched the pillow, and clutched it to my chest and thought, that I didn't even know what a psychologist meant. And I shouted, *no*, determined not to cry no matter what.

For a moment, I forgot the fear and anxiety. For a moment, I forgot the lightning and thunder and decided to play with my soccer ball. Yes! I shouted and clapped my hands and jumped off the bed and ran to take out the ball from the closet. But then I froze, alarmed, as if someone invisible caught me from behind. And I stood there staring at the closet door and remembered that only a few days ago, I broke two of your geranium pots when I played ball in the room, and you were so angry I thought you'd never forgive me. I wet my bed every night, and Father grumbled and grumbled. And with these thoughts, the sudden surge of energy left my body, and I banged my fists on the closet door and kicked it with my foot and hurt my big toe and shouted shit! And I didn't even care that I promised you never to say that word. I found no relief. Only the rain was beating on the roof, and it sounded like horses' hooves stamping above my head. And I was sure the world was going to end any moment now, but you weren't there to protect me.

Angry with the rain and angry with my father and angry with you, furious with the entire dark universe, I took out a big sheet of paper and my crayons and crouched on the floor on my knees and drew a figure of a man who resembled the man in the picture on your little bedside table, and above the picture, I scribbled a name in black letters. Then I went to your desk and opened the drawer and took out a pair of sharp scissors that you warned me never to touch, and gouged the eyes and cut off *his* nose and mouth and ears. Then violently, I beheaded *him*. I plucked each finger separately, and severed the right arm, then the left. Then I removed the legs and the feet, and I cut the body into four equal parts. And when I finished to gouge and to cut and to tear and to sever, I scooped up the pieces and tossed them into the air and blew on them with all my might and clapped my hands and shouted, "Go away, already!" And I looked up and saw the parts of the mutilated body hovering above me, and I covered my head with my hands, and then I saw *him* flutter to the floor and lie there. And *his* empty eyes stared at me, and the hole of the mouth smirked at me in an impudent and leering way, and my whole body shuddered. So I picked up the pieces one by one, ran to the bathroom, threw them down the toilet, flushed the water, and said, *there*, and my heart was threatening to burst from my body. I went back to the living room and took the fuzzy red blanket from the sofa and wrapped it around myself, and sat down and pressed my knees to my chest, and tried to imagine myself as a fuzzy and big and red bug. But it wasn't any good to pretend because I remained a little boy. And then a blinding white flash flooded the room, and I squeezed my eyes shut and clapped my hands to my ears and felt the impact shaking my body. And I said aloud, "It's only a thunder," and I tried to whistle, but I couldn't move my lips. I looked again at the clock and saw that it was only seven and you weren't going to be back for two hours yet.

So, I wrapped myself tighter in the red blanket and dropped my head on the back of the sofa and closed my eyes and tried to breathe slowly in and out, in and out through the nose softly, like Dr. Shoham taught me to do when I didn't feel good. But it didn't help, and my mind was swimming with images of strange, dark, and horrifying scenes. I saw a shapeless and huge body coming right at me from the silence of the Rocky Hill where Big Micha's body is buried, and I shook my head to shatter the image and sucked air into my lungs and opened my eyes wide and vowed to myself never to close them again until you were home. And the confusion in my head became enormous because as long as I remember myself, I heard people say that Big Micha wasn't buried on Rocky Hill at all because his body was blown to pieces while he parachuted over Jerusalem toward the Ammunition Hill during the Six-Day War and he couldn't be identified. In those days, I couldn't understand why the name Micha Oren was engraved in the big stone on Rocky Hill. They said it was symbolic, but what does a seven-year-old boy know about things being symbolic?

Oh, Mother, I was so scared just like that day when everyone in the kibbutz went to the Rocky Hill (I went because you had insisted even though Father was against it) and gathered around a stone engraved with the name Micha Oren, and they were all so deathly serious and grim, and their heads hung down as if they were ashamed of something. They wore dark glasses and looked like blind people look in pictures, and suddenly I had a strong urge to giggle, but I didn't giggle and didn't even smile because I knew you'd be furious with me, and I wouldn't be able to explain to you that even though I giggled, it wasn't because something funny was going on there. No, I definitely didn't think that things were funny. They were anything but funny. And I saw people's lips move ever so little, and I didn't understand what they were mumbling without a voice, and then I heard Old Gara reading from the Bible, *'Abraham,' God called. 'Yes, Lord,' he replied. 'Take with you your only son, yes, Isaac, whom you love so much, and go to the land of Moriah and sacrifice him there as a burnt offering upon one of the mountains which I will point out to you.'* I didn't believe a word of this horrible story even when Dahlia, my favorite teacher, read it to us in Bible class. And I hated Abraham and pitied Isaac, and to my horror, I began to cry in class. The children looked at me with sort of wonder mixed with mockery except for Nati she too cried a little and pretended as if she only had the sniffles. And Dahlia caressed my head and told me to go wash my face and have a drink of water and not to be so sad because it is only a story. Remember Dahlia? Big and soft and very gentle, always raking her hair with chalk-stained fingers like a plow in a wheat field, and sometimes when I daydreamed of you or watched Nati's legs, Dahlia would stop at my desk and say, "Micha, try to concentrate." And I never understood how she knew that I wasn't. The next day, after she read to us this horrible story, you came to school and went with Dahlia to the teacher's room and you stayed there forever. I hid behind the school and waited for you to come out, and when you came out, your face was white and worried and your eyes swollen and red and your legs hardly carried you. I was sure that you were ill, so I was worried and was ill, and I vomited among the pomegranate trees. I stood behind the school, leaning against its wall, and cried. And you never said a word to me about that meeting, and I never asked. I knew that you liked Dahlia because from all the people who wanted to sit with you at lunch or dinner, you always chose to sit with Dahlia, and when I asked you why, you said you had a lot to talk about.

And on that Memorial Day in the Rocky Hill, oh, Mother, I wanted to run away from there. It was so spooky. The air hummed with whispers and hisses and echoes and faint cries and sighs, and I was sure that in a moment, evil spirits would attack me. And I longed to hide among the rocks, catch tiny snails, dig for earthworms, and watch how the butterflies tease the flowers; so I looked down at my feet and vowed to myself not to think, when suddenly I saw a small turtle, pathetic and helpless, lying on his back on the grass, feebly flailing its legs in the air in a futile effort to turn over. I wanted to bend down and help it, but I couldn't move because my hand was squeezed inside my father's huge and sweating palm, and my head swayed. So I looked up at the trees and listened to the birds sing and I felt better. Suddenly there was a commotion; people were running toward me. My father dropped my hand, and bending down quickly, I turned the turtle over and whispered, "Run away, little turtle, run before they'll kill you." And when

I looked up, I saw you lying on the grass, and your eyes were closed, and your face was white as chalk, and you looked like a broken doll. Father was kneeling beside you; then he picked you up and carried you in his arms all the way back to our house. And I ran behind him, and he laid you on the bed and shut the door in my face.

The night of that memorial service, my father sat on my bed for a long time and was very silent, and suddenly I heard myself ask, "Where do we go after we die?" And Father said that after death, we don't go anywhere, and I asked, "Are you sure?" And he said, "Yes, I'm sure. Who put such absurd ideas in your head?" And I insisted that after we die, we meet in heaven, and Father sighed and kissed my forehead. His serious eyes were sad and very tired, and I thought I heard him mutter under his breath, "Rita, Rita, what are you doing to the child?" And he kissed me again. "Good night, son," he said. And at that moment, I loved him terribly, so I put my arms around his neck, and he hugged me tight to his massive chest just like I had seen him hug you.

That night, I couldn't fall asleep, and I tossed and turned and counted to a hundred and listened to the frogs and crickets outside and pressed my fingers to my eyes until I saw strange shapes and colors. I even tried to sing under my blanket, but nothing could chase away the dead from the Rocky Hill, and my mind was alert to the slightest move or sound from your bedroom. Maybe you'll come to kiss me good night and hold me tight, and the night will be soft and quiet. Nevertheless, in the morning, the sheets were soaked, and the hateful stink of urine greeted the new day, and the cold morning air cut through my wet pajamas. But I hadn't slept all night, so how had it happened? *Don't cry; take hold of yourself,* I commanded myself.

The next day, you were unlike yourself. You refused to see your friends and ignored my father, and when you spoke to me, your voice was flat and monotonous. Father left you alone, and your friends shook their heads and clicked their tongues and said, "Poor Rita." And I attached myself to you like a leech, and you said, "Michal'e, don't you have anything better to do than follow me around all day? You're driving me nuts." But I tugged at your hands and laughed in a tone that even I could tell was most unpleasant, and I told you stories about school and my friends and about Old Gara, who took me to see how a calf is being born. "So much blood, Mommy, so much blood." But the cow wasn't scared, only licked and licked her calf with a tongue so pink and large and rough until her baby was smooth and shining. And he tripped and fell and got up and again tripped until Old Gara picked it up and put it next his mother's udder, and he sucked and pulled and made funny noises. And Old Gara let me stroke its head, and its head was warm and damp and sticky, so wonderful." And all you said was, "Michal'e, don't shout, I'm not deaf." And I got confused because I wasn't aware that I was shouting,—well, maybe my voice was a little louder than usual,—and I was going to tell you how much I loved Nati, but I didn't because you weren't listening. And I felt as if I were invisible, unnecessary by the world, and I turned away from you because, at age seven, I hadn't understood the meaning of the weird gathering at Rocky Hill, and I knew that Big Micha's body wasn't there because it had been torn to pieces and couldn't be identified. I wished then that I knew what identified meant, and although I had wanted to ask many questions, I didn't because every time the words were almost there, my lips got numb and I couldn't utter a sound from fear I wouldn't find the right words.

I also knew then that before I was born, you wanted to marry Big Micha because you were in love with him, and I wondered if you had felt about Big Micha the way I felt about Nati. And although this question often occupied my thoughts, I could never really make up my mind about it because grown-ups, in my opinion, were full of dark secrets, and I felt as though I were living in a place where everyone but me knew an important secret. But no one ever said it aloud, at least not while I was present, not even you.

When did I learn about you and Big Micha? It seemed that I always knew, and I remembered in particular one summer night when the moon was full, and it had been awfully hot and humid. You had left the door to your bedroom wide open, and I was lying in my bed awake, sweating in the sheets, when suddenly I heard you cry and say that you should have married Big Micha. Father answered that Micha wasn't the marrying kind, that he had the soul of a gypsy. I didn't understand, but I shut my eyes tight as if I were waiting for a blow. And then you said something that sounded very strange to me. "You don't always marry the one you truly love," was exactly what you'd said, and after that, there was silence. And I thought that what you'd said didn't make any sense at all and that maybe you're even lying because I loved Nati best of all the girls in the kibbutz, and I was sure that I would marry her as soon as I was through with my army service, perhaps even sooner, because when I thought of Nati, I felt a quiver of pleasure throughout my whole body. Nati's legs were beautiful, her hair had the color of your hair, her eyes were huge and brown, almond shaped, and I had no doubt then that I was going to marry her. And later in that night, I heard you say, "I shouldn't have given in to his romantic talk about living together." "Rita," he would say, "what difference does it make what people say?" "But it made a difference to me, and I shouldn't have listened to him, especially after I learned about my condition." "Rita, Rita," Father cajoled, "it's enough. I'm begging you, it's enough." But you only laughed a terrible laugh, or maybe you were crying. And I didn't hear any more because I jammed my fingers into my ears and saw the walls of my room moving, closing in on me. At that moment, Mother, I hated you. And in my dream that night, I was crushing Big Micha's skull with a big stone, and I smashed and smashed. But his skull wouldn't break, and his mouth whispered something I didn't understand, and I raised the stone to strike again, but instead of a stone, my hand was gripping a hand, and the hand was your hand. I woke up terrified and crying, and you came running from your room and got into my bed and gathered my body into your arms, and didn't seem to mind the stench of urine. I clung to you and sobbed, "Mommy, I had a bad dream." And you said "It's all right, grown-ups have bad dreams too. Hush, my darling, I am here now. You don't have to be afraid anymore. There are no bad dreams now, hush." You cuddled me to your body and sang to me in your small, sad voice song after song, and you made my fear melt away. I fell asleep pressing my face into your breasts.

And I hated to be called Little Micha. I was the tallest in my class, and every time I passed the hall mirror, I saw a broad-shouldered boy with tight red curls and a freckled face that I detested but which grown-ups thought cut. My one consolation was my eyes. Green, like yours. Big Micha's eyes, I was told, were brown like my father's because it's natural for brothers to have the same eye color. But most of all, I hated my hair. I hated it so much that one day, when I came from school, I went straight to the kitchen cabinet where you kept a bottle of olive oil and emptied the entire content on my head, and when I looked in the bathroom mirror, I clapped my hands and shouted, "Magic! Magic!" because my curly hair turned straight and brown like my father's. But the olive oil dripped into my eyes, and I rubbed my eyelids with my fists, and the world looked like a messy jigsaw puzzle. And then I saw you standing at the door (I didn't even hear you come home) and pretended to ignore you, but in my heart, I wondered why you hadn't said anything or got angry. You only watched me silently, your face whiter than usual. Finally, almost blind, the olive oil burning my eyes, I went to you for help.

And you didn't say a word; you only took me by the hand back to the bathroom and washed my head and rinsed my eyes. And then I was standing between your knees while you rubbed my head with a towel until it felt as if the skin of my scalp were coming off together with my hateful hair. And you cupped my face between the palms of your hands and your eyes were two green stars, and you said, "Michal'e, this is the way God had made you. It's important to like yourself as you are." But I insisted angrily, "I want to look like my father." And you rose from the chair, still holding my face between the palms of your hands, and said, "King David had red hair, and he was the most handsome man in the Bible." And I felt my anger rising and pulled away from you, and while tears were choking my throat, I screamed at you that I didn't care about King David's hair and that your hair wasn't red either. At that moment, you were standing with your back against the window, the afternoon sun was behind you, and its yellow rays were making your hair gold. And I said, "Like sunlight, your hair is like sunlight. Only mine is red." Digesting. And I saw the green of your eyes turning hard and gray and your hands left my cheeks, and you said, "You're lucky to have red hair. Big Micha had red hair, and he was as beautiful as King David." At that moment, I knew that he would always be between us. "Big Micha is dead!" I shouted in your face. "Dead people are not lucky. Their bodies are torn to pieces, and no one knows where they're buried. That's what happens to people with red hair." And I saw how you almost stopped breathing and your face blanched, and for a moment, you stood there speechless. Then you whispered, "My god, what are you saying?" And I screamed, "Old Gara said that it brings bad luck to name a boy after his dead uncle. I heard him say so. I heard him say it many times, to many people. I heard him say it to my father!" And your face turned this awful shade of purple red, and you raised your hand. And for the first time in my life, I was sure

27

you were going to hit me across the face, and I stuck my head between my shoulders, waiting for the blow, but you lowered your hand.

"Gara," you spat his name, "I should have known, the old fool. You shouldn't listen to what people say." "I don't listen!" I screamed. "I hear. I hear them whisper. They whisper all the time!" And you grabbed me by the shoulders, and my eyes, open to their limits, were in your eyes, and my anger choked me. A sort of wired smile hovered on your face, and you said, "Big Micha was a wonderful man," and you let go of my shoulders, and I released my breath and let go of your eyes. You said in your soft, sad voice, "My beautiful man," and you touched my hair. But your gaze was far away, and your eyes were full of longing. I swallowed my tears, tensed my body, and thought in my heart, *no, I'm not a baby. I didn't cling or cry—as long as I could help it.* I turned away from you and stuck my hands in my pockets, and went to play with my friends, but on the way, I threw a few stones at Sam the Cat and scored a point this time. Sam ran away howling like mad, but I didn't feel triumphant. I only walked aimlessly along the narrow path, hitting the shrubs and kicking the stones and praying not to be seen by anyone. And I thought to myself that you said many things I didn't understand, and I wanted so much to be sure they were good things because your voice was soft and your face so pretty, but I loved your eyes above all. They were green and clear and, at times, kind of blue or gray. And sometimes I would catch you looking strangely, and your gaze would be focused on something I couldn't see, something beyond my head, and you would be smiling this special, longing smile. Then I would run to you, put my arms around your waist, and press my face into your belly, longing to tell you not to be sad, Mama, because I love you and I'd take care of you. And you would caress my hair, and your touch would send waves and tingles throughout my entire body, and you would say that you loved me more than anyone else in the whole world. Then why would I feel that you were talking to someone who wasn't there? Mother, Mother. And you never called me Little Micha. You called me Michal'e, and I wondered if it was because you knew how mad it made me to be called Little Micha. It drove me insane when someone would ruffle my hair and pinch my cheek and say *'Big Micha all the way. The eyes are Rita's, still, a spitting image. Big Micha was a brave man. You're brave too, right?'*

At moments like that, I would feel my anger consuming me like a fire. My breathing would stop, and I would stand frozen. My hands would curl into tight fists ready to punch and do something nasty like I did that day when, after school, I went to the cowshed where Old Gara worked. I liked going to the cowshed in the winter, but you would grumble and pull a face and say, "Don't come near me, Michal'e. You stink like a cow. Again, you went to the cowshed? What are you looking for there? Why don't you play with friends?" But I didn't care if I stunk like a cow. It was friendly there and warm and smelly and dirty and steamy, and Old Gara would let me drink milk right from the cow's udder. I never told you that because I knew you'd be annoyed and preach to me for days about viruses, bacteria, and health. Sometimes Old Gara would tell me jokes I didn't understand, like the joke about the farmer and his cow and something about love and tits, and when I asked him, "What's tits?" that knocked Old Gara out. He began to laugh like a maniac and collapsed onto the milking bench. I was afraid he'd die laughing, and suddenly I found myself laughing and mooing like I had never laughed and mooed until my stomach hurt and tears rolled down my cheeks. Oh, Mother, it felt wonderful. So what if I hadn't understood the joke? And I was still laughing and mooing and jumping about the barn when suddenly I noticed Old Gara glaring at me as if I'd stolen something, so I stopped dancing and cocked my head and asked what. And Old Gara said, "They ought to tell you. It isn't right. You look exactly like him, and why not. It's absolutely normal for a boy to look like his . . ." The rest of the words hung over me like dirty laundry, and my heart began to pound, and the blood rushed to my face. I screamed, "I look like my father!" Then I bent down and stuck my hand in a manure pile and picked up a handful of cow shit and threw it in Gara's face. I ran out of the cowshed and hid in the granary. And there, in the granary, surrounded by whispers, I had a huge asthma attack, and I spun for hours on a white cloud.

In the evening, when Father asked how I could behave in such a disgusting manner, I glared into his eyes and remained silent. What could I say? Tell him about the rage? The despair? The whispers? The double-meaning glances that are thrown at me? "Why, Michal'e? Why?" you pleaded. I wanted to run to you and scream, "Love me like you love Big Micha," but I couldn't. I felt like a rag was stuffed into my throat, and I couldn't even whisper. That evening, I received my first thrashing from my father, and you sat watching, not saying a word. But your eyes were gray—like the stones on Rocky Hill—and wounded, and your hands were tightly clenched in your lap. During the beating, I felt nothing.

Later that same night, when you thought I was asleep, I heard my father say, "I think we should tell him. It's better for the kid to know." You shouted no. And Father asked, "When, Rita?" And you said, your voice full of dread, "Not yet, he's too young. He won't understand." (Did you really think that I didn't understand? You were very naive, Mama.) And Father said, "It's time, Rita. He isn't a baby anymore." And you began to cry. "No, Eli. God no. He'll never forgive me. He even hates his own name, and he'll hate me." (How is it possible that you hadn't known, Mama, that I could never hate you? How could you disappear like that? Betray me? Let me grow up without you? Have a bar mitzvah without you? Go into the army to become a paratrooper without you?) And Father said, and his voice came from somewhere deep inside his belly, "Rita, Rita, what am I going to do with you?" And that night, when I was waiting for sleep to come and take me, I thought to myself that maybe it's better to be an orphan, like this boy Copperfield you'd been reading to me about. So strong was the image of being without you stamped upon my mind that I jumped up and threw away the red blanket and shouted no and ran to the window, and for a moment, I stood there rooted to the floor and shut my eyes tight and listened with all my might. *Yes,* I shouted and clapped my hands and flung the window open and realized that the storm has blown itself out, and the silence was as complete as if God had turned the whole world off.

I stayed for a while by the open window, sniffed the wetness and savored the stillness, then I went to your bedroom, and I sat on your bed, and my eyes fell on the picture of the soldier with the red hair and found myself face-to-face with my own smile. And with my eyes locked on the picture, I squeezed my body under your blanket and hid my face in your pillow and hissed venomously at the man in the picture, "I'm glad you're dead. I hate you. I hate you." But the truth was I didn't feel hate for anyone, and the silence was soothing, and I was so tired, and soon the buzz in my head became vague as if it came from a great distance or belonged to someone else, and I turned my face to the wall and squirmed deeper under the blanket where it was dark and warm and smelled like your body and hair, and my eyes closed with pleasure. Suddenly I heard a noise. Someone was coming. I bolted out of the bed and was running. "Mommy! Mommy!" I shouted and clapped my hands. I jerked the door wide open. It wasn't you who was standing there, smiling. "I promised, didn't I?" said my little friend, Nati, and walked right past me into the living room. "Why are you wearing pajamas, Michal'e?" she asked. "Are you ill?" I didn't answer; I only gazed at her as if she were a miracle. "I saw a million snails and earthworms by the dining hall,"

Nati said. "Really?" I said and caught my breath, feeling the shreds of the storm in my head retreating, as if being chased away by this little bit of a girl. "Wonderful puddles," Nati said, "everywhere." Her brilliant huge almond-shaped eyes were fixed on my face, urging, teasing, and I knew she was up to something mischievous. I looked away from her down at the floor and said, "I was scared of the storm." And she said, "Me too." I looked at her and asked, "You really were afraid?" And she said, "Ah ha." And I watched how the rain dripped from her hair into her eyelashes, into her shoulders, into her blouse, into her shoes, into every part of her body, and rainwater ran down her legs into the floor, and she was sucking out the moisture from a bunch of hair between her lips, and my body relaxed, and I laughed. "You're lying, you love storms, you told me so yourself," but she ignored my words and said, "You know, Michal'e, I saw a turtle on the way." And I asked, "A big turtle?" She chuckled, "So-so," and suddenly we were laughing and jumping and shouting, and making a big wet mess on your spotless carpet. And I felt my pajama bottom slipping down my legs toward the floor, and I caught it just in time. And that's how we were when you came home. Out of the corner of my eye, I saw you standing at the open door, watching. Your eyes were their deepest green, and you said in your soft, sad voice, "Michal'e, my beautiful boy," and my heart leaped with joy.

How did you leave me, Mother? How did you leave me? You pointed the rifle toward your heart and squeezed the trigger. Didn't you know that you were everything and everything in me goes back to you? They say it was an accident, and they say you didn't know the gun was loaded. What do they really know about you? And they're still whispering . . . always whispering.

SORROW HAS NO VOICE

Where were your arms
when I was still twined
in webs of dreams?
When I reached out to your
tiny arms in primordial thirst?

You turned away your head
and closed the door behind your back
and I didn't know yet
how to cry your name.

For years I wandered
in fields
gathering dry leaves
breathing the scent
of decaying flowers.

The poppies froze
the daffodils emitted
an evil laugh.
You were harsh
as a fruitless soil.

Now you are dead
and I am still searching for you
lost
among shadows
of
frozen
poppies.

ILANA HALEY

AT THE END OF THE PARTY

Suddenly in the dumb evening, I saw light,
I found a refuge in love.

But at the end of the party,
silent as a thief,
Loneliness crept back
and sunk her talons into me;
calm, malignant, sucking,
smiling her irony—
you belong to me.

From the agony of separation,
my heart turned white as vapor cloud.
From grief that
descended upon me like an
evil angel
I observed the staggering immensity
of the experience.
From within the process of galloping decay
I cast a last fading glance toward
past fertility.

It was so decreed
that
I remain
a slave
to
love

SAY THE WORDS

Violent twilights clasp granite sky
Quick! Command the silence, if this storm lasts
The city will collapse
The plants, man, beast—
The life.
Silence the night
Place your hand on brow of boiling earth
Breathe into its failing heart
Say the words that only you can utter
Smooth shards of stars with silent sigh.
To you alone the soul is yearning
To you and to the softness of your touch that like
A feather pass upon the lashes of my mind
Say the words that only you can utter
Bring back the glory of the past.
My love, so virgin, will embrace your essence
I'll dwell inside the quiet of your light
With lightest hand then, you'll smooth my spirit
And with your breath as light as zephyr
Bring back the spring.

FRAGMENTS

The excitement at that time
Was of a different sort,
Weaving inside weaving
Slowly knitting a carpet of utopia,
An excited anticipation of the
Stirring presence,
And sun, so much sun
Even so, it was an excitement
Of a different sort, not
Gut-wrenching, not hilarious,
Quiet
With a long breath—
Perhaps with a hidden trembling
Of the hands.

*

Through lemon orchards
Through inflamed sunrises
We did not go in vain.
Even though our faces
Were lifted to heaven
And stars flickered in our eyes
We knew that the desert of bones
Lay only a few steps from us.

*

The road was arduous
Sometimes we were lost
Sometimes the
Lack of knowledge
Overtook us
We forgot those
That we should have remembered
We remembered those
We should have forgot.

*

All that day
We were consumed by the fury
We did not discuss, did not forget
We closed ourselves
To all possibilities
We died for a moment.
Our intention was good.

*

When it came
It didn't shine, didn't
Embrace, didn't soar,
Didn't burst into song,
It penetrated, harsh and
Moaning, exuding an odor of
Sweat, bringing with it
A sort of opaque memory of
Shame and a faraway image
Of something that once, for
Some reason, was alike and
Known only through
A complete absence
Of knowing.

*

Suddenly it vanished
As if it never was
And we were not entirely sure
If it was bad or worse
Fragments of its memories
Were with us all along
But when we met, we weren't
Clear if we could bring it home.
We argued, showing dimmed recall,
Escaping lack of choice that
Comes with absent confidence
And lack of knowing voice
We were exuberant, accusing
We uttered bitter words,
But even so, we didn't know
What or whom to curse.
We were enraged we were upset
We threw embittered words
Yet, nothing could have changed the fact
That we remained alone.
Our parents died and those who live
Are vanishing each day
How could we blame those who
Had gone to look for farther bay?

*

We are tired.
What more can we demand from time?
Another toxin, spiritual marijuana?
I will stay right here until
I tell you otherwise
And you?
Please look for me.

*

Tell the right lies. I know all the lies.
If you understand, good, if your decision
Is to pass under me as under a bridge
I will not forgive and not, not forgive,—
In a moment, the millennium will be
Behind us, now is the time to sum up.

*

So, I am asking you,
What is left
Of my moment?
And what is left
Of yours?

*

Through the window, now
I see a piece of sky wearing
A bridal veil of calm light
And a fragrant autumn rolls
A pleasant presence
Between its cool fingers,
Stunning the city in a halo of
Autumn's shades
And all is natural.—
Every season is
Natural.

STRAWBERRY OMELET

(MARTA)

All that night, the rain fell thick and insistent.

All that night, Marta was deep into her reveries; the voices humming far and near, high and low; the visions clear and sharp, others as pale as shreds of fog.

Marta's eyes are closed, but she is not asleep. She is afraid to sleep. Devoured by cancer, drowning in morphine, she lay in her bed under the window, listening to the rain, holding her breath, postponing the pain each breath cost.

The rain stopped at dawn. She saw the sunrise in her mind's eye:

Red sun bursting from rain-saturated clouds. Large drops of water glistening boldly on the branches of the cypress trees, balancing for a moment, then falling, disappearing into the cracks of the parched earth.

Her pain is dim and distant. Her imagination hovers in the kibbutz, in the world. She is digging deep into the archives of memories, sunk into the world of images. Now she sees the teacher Dahlia meet with Anna near the Children's House.

"Thank God it rained," Anna says. "I was getting worried. Another drought would have been a disaster."

"I must hurry," Dahlia says. "The children are all over the place getting filthy, looking for snails and earthworms."

And Marta sees Anna smile and smooth with a calm hand a bunch of white hair from her forehead. "Relax, Dahlia," she says. "The children will get wet anyway. Besides, it's good for them. You mustn't worry so much. You already have an ulcer. Look! What a beautiful day. It'll probably rain again this afternoon."

But Dahlia puckers her forehead, narrows her eyes, sighs, and says, "Anna, you always know everything." And she adds quickly, "See you," and they disappear.

Now she imagines Ezra, her husband, on his way to the sheep pen, meeting with Eli, the kibbutz mechanist.

"A beautiful day, Ezra. Did you hear the deluge last night?" she hears Eli say to her husband. "What do you think? Will it be a good year?"

"We live and hope," Ezra mutters.

"Lots of grass for the sheep. What do you say, Ezra?"

"Yah." Ezra allows himself to be cajoled into a stingy smile. "Lots of good grass for the sheep this year."

"How is Marta this morning?" Eli asks.

With her mind's eye, Marta watches her husband, trying not to miss a word. What will he say? But Ezra only shakes his head. Are those tears in his eyes? She isn't certain. Her imagination follows her distancing husband, his hands deep inside his pockets, his shoulders hunched.

"Ezra, straighten up," she says aloud, startled by her own voice.

Near the dining hall, she sees children playing boisterously, chasing one another, sloshing in the mud, jumping into puddles of water, shrieking with laughter as they gather little rain critters, which had appeared overnight. Dahlia, the teacher, is beside herself.

"Little Micha," she admonishes, *"you'll catch cold! Nati, look how wet and muddy you are. Daphna, let go of those worms, you're crushing the poor creatures."*

"Nati, Nati, look, I've got five snails," she hears Little Micha say to Nati.

"Little Micha, look at the rainbow!" cries Nati.

"Nati, my little angel," Marta whispers. She places her hands on her heart and, with a great effort, opens her eyes. The shutters are shut, the curtains drawn. She does not want the sun. Light is of no use to her. She lies inert as if dead. Only her eyes, two green dots in a gray face, shine feverishly in the dimness of her room. "Where is Ezra?" she mutters then smiles. She knows where he is: in the fields tending the sheep, dreaming of young women with heavy breasts. How she misses the green pastures, the endless wide meadows. The smell of the earth used to intoxicate her, fill her with a sensuous pleasure. The land is in her soul, in her body, her decaying body.

How lucky is Ezra, her silly husband, which like all other men loses his head to the sight of big breasts and full thighs. The thought brings a spasm of familiar pain in the pit of her gut. She never quite understood why she had married him in the first place, except that they were both young and enkindled by a dream. And he had been so handsome. In the little Polish town where they were born, he had been a teacher, respected, and admired by everyone. They met one summer at a Zionist group meeting, and he fell in love with her, or so he said. Without examining her own feelings, she went with him to Palestine. It was enough for her that they shared the same vision—Israel! Later she thought that Ezra had never had a dream, not even when they first joined the kibbutz. He had become the sheep expert while, for thirty years, she took care of the infants. In the beginning, they fought, or to be precise, she fought and he remained silent.

But with time, and in spite the lack of understanding, a careful love blossomed between them, even tender, and although lovemaking between them was awkward, and without satisfaction, she continued to make love with him without passion, yet unable to stop. She was hit by feelings of guilt, and resentment toward him as if they had missed some great opportunity. But she also knew that they were carrying between them a heavy weight that only the two of them together were able to carry.

A few days earlier, she asked Ezra to hand her a mirror.

"You don't need a mirror, you look fine," he'd grumbled. But Marta insisted; so he brought the small hand mirror from the bathroom, laid it by her hand, and quickly left the room. She picked it up, hardly able to hold it. For a moment, she looked only at her hand. She shuddered. All her life, she was proud of her lovely hands, and now she saw dry skin, yellow and spotted. She was looking at a dead hand. She wanted to cry and decided not to look at her face. "Never mind," she muttered, dropped the mirror, and shut her eyes.

Now, as always, she was thinking about her youngest daughter, Iris, who constantly hovered at the edge of her consciousness. Iris had never been like other children. Iris face, since she was a baby, was clouded. Iris, who never smiled, never played. She asked for nothing and accepted nothing. She seemed to be locked in a tight, lightless place. Marta remembered how difficult it was to love Iris, what a tremendous effort it took even to communicate with the sullen, dark little girl, that silently came out of her womb, and silently remained. Iris never once crawled onto her lap or even cried. Sometimes during the day, Marta would go to the Toddlers' House and look at her daughter sitting alone in the corner, her eyes gazing blankly into the distance. In moments like that, Marta wanted to scream. Later in kindergarten, the children ignored her. At school, she sat alone. The children named her the Weird One.

The silent girl grew into a frozen young woman. Marta's heart burned with pain and guilt, the tears choking her throat as she watched Iris's empty face and wooden movements. Despite many wakeful nights, she, who knew all about children, didn't understand what was wrong with her daughter. Sometimes at night, she would try to talk to Ezra about it. But Ezra locked himself inside himself. "I don't understand children psychology," he would say, and she angrily blamed him for not supporting her, for not caring enough. And then she would be ashamed of herself for the rage she unloaded on him, for she saw his eyes mist in pain and frustration as he watched their five-year-old gazing blankly into the distance, her eyes dark glass.

When Iris was eighteen years old, she slashed her wrists.

That day, like any other day, Marta was working in the Children's House. She was bathing Guy, Dahlia's little boy, when Anna came running in. "Marta!" she gasped. "It's Iris! Let's go! Hurry!"

Marta clasped little Guy to her chest and leaned against the wall, letting out a low sound. Anna took the baby from her arms.

"It's bad." Anna's voice came to Marta like an echo from her own belly. She saw Iris dead. Panic gripped her, and for a long moment, she was paralyzed with terror.

"Marta!" Anna shook her shoulders. "Marta, it's Iris! Marta, do you understand?"

Marta came out of her stupor. "Ezra," she whispered. "Does Ezra know?"

"We sent Eli to fetch him from the field." Anna caught her hand. "Let's go!" she said.

When she saw Iris lying on the bed, red bandages on her wrists, her panic vanished. Her daughter needed her.

"Iris?" She shook her daughter's shoulder lightly. "Iris?"

Iris didn't respond.

"She's in shock." She heard Anna's voice from somewhere in the distance.

"Iris, it's me, Marta." Iris always called her Marta, never Mother. She bent down and kissed her daughter's forehead. It felt cold and dry. Marta held her daughter until the wailing of the ambulance penetrated their privacy. Her body tightened like that of a wounded animal.

On the way to the hospital, for the first time in her life, she pleaded with God.

For forty-eight hours, Marta sat by her daughter's bed. Her two other children came to see their sister; but mostly they sat with their mother, holding her hand, trying to comfort her. She didn't hear or see them. Her eyes didn't leave Iris's face. All her senses were completely focused on the inert face, as if she was begging her daughter to allow her to share her loneliness.

"What did I do wrong?" she asked herself repeatedly. But she knew the truth.

During her two-day watch at Iris's bedside, Marta grew to love her daughter in a new way, a soft love,—a love that she never felt for her daughter. In sleep Iris's face lost its morbidity, her brow was smooth and her skin clear. And Marta noticed how long and thick Iris's eyelashes were. She thought of her daughter's eyes, huge almond-shaped brown, now closed.

Why did Iris reject life? She asked herself, tears running down her cheeks. "Iris, my child," she whispered, "speak to me."

Iris opened her eyes as if she heard her mother's words, and for one moment, Marta perceived a depth of pain that she had never seen there before. The corners of Iris's mouth turned down, and Marta couldn't tell if it was a smile or an expression of pain. Iris's hand moved, and Marta covered it with her own trembling hand.

"Mother," Iris said, "I am going to have a baby." Then she closed her eyes.

Iris, who had never called her mother, who had always been a mystery to her, became real. She sat there for hours, watching

Iris's face, softly stroking her hand. Doctors and nurses came and went away. Her friends from the kibbutz brought her food and drinks, trying to persuade her to lie down and rest. And Marta made a tremendous effort to smile at everyone but didn't answer. She didn't remove her eyes from Iris's face and continued to stroke her hand. The thoughts were beating wildly in her head. Who did Iris sleep with? Who is responsible for her pregnancy? Was she raped? Will she ever have the courage to ask? And if she'd ask, how would Iris respond? Frightened, she reined her thoughts, tears burning in her throat.

In the evening, Ezra found her curled up on the bed, her face on the pillow next to Iris's head, both of them in deep sleep. He stood there looking at them for a long time; lines of sorrow and love were etched deep in his face, his heart moaning in his chest. Suddenly, unexpectedly, Marta opened her eyes. She sat up. "I fell asleep." She smiled at him confusedly, her cheeks turning red. Softly Ezra stroked her head, then bent, and kissed her lips. "Shah . . . Sleep," he whispered and hurried to leave the room.

Through the open door, she saw him leaning against the hallway wall, his shoulders shaking and—he was weeping like a child.

Seven months later, Iris gave birth to a healthy little girl. She named her Natanya, meaning "a gift from God."

A sad smile illuminated for a moment Marta's ravished face. She remembered the night she conceived Iris. It was raining. Phosphorescent snakes of lightning zigzagged across the sky. A wild wind shook the shutters. She tossed, unable to sleep. Ezra, in the other bed, was sleeping calmly, his breath coming in a soft whistle through his slightly opened lips.

Suddenly she threw off her blanket. "Ezra," she called. "Ezra!"

Ezra's eyes fluttered. "Ha? Ha? What is it?" he muttered then resumed his sleep.

She opened the door, welcoming the rain into their small room. The wind whistled in her ears, whipping her hair across her face into her eyes. Within seconds, she was drenched all over, her hair dripping. Something hard inside her melted; her skin shuddered with yearning and sensuality, as if the rain was the lover she always yearned for. She spread her arms and lifted her face, letting the rain caress her skin, lustily breathing its wet-earth scent.

"Marta, for God's sake, closes the door. You'll catch your death!" She heard Ezra's voice.

"Ezra," she called, "come, it's so exciting."

But Ezra only grumbled and covered his head with the blanket.

She stood smiling, hearing her mother's voice saying the same words. "Marta, for God's sake, you'll catch your death, child. Close the door." But her mother's voice full of love, and when Marta came back into the house, her mother, who too had loved to stand in the rain, was waiting for her with a glass of hot milk and a towel. But most vividly, she remembered her mother's embracing smile and the little house where she grew and her father and someone caressing her head and the feeling of belonging and calmness.

After a while, she came back into the room, took off her soaking nightgown, and rubbed her hair with a towel. She looked at Ezra. She was surprised to see his eyes open, his hands clasped behind his head—he was watching her.

"What is it? What are you staring at?" she asked, feeling suddenly shy.

"You are beautiful," he said.

She giggled, feeling like a young girl. He had never said she looked beautiful. Not when he proposed to her, not when they got married, not when their children were born. His unexpected words made her tremble with anticipation. It has been years since her body wakened with desire. Now she wanted to be swept away by her mounting excitement. She dropped the towel then, trembling, got into his bed, hoping this time it will be like in her dreams, like love should be. But as usual, he hurried to take her. And while he was moaning and sweating above her, she listened to the rain splattering against the windows and fancied that her soul left her body there on the bed and soared. She imagined herself being carried away on a cloud, singing the songs of her youth.

Afterward, she stayed awake and listened to the wind. Her excitement at Ezra's words, "You're beautiful," melted away and was replaced by a deep loneliness.

That night, Iris was conceived.

Marta was forty-two when she conceived Iris, Ezra forty-eight and looking so young. Where his face was smooth and tanned, hers was dry and lined like a spider web. His belly was strong and hard, hers sagged from childbearing. His hair was thick and shiny, her own stricken with gray and thinning. But, she consoled herself, his soul is dull and his heart timid, while hers was vivacious and daring.

Tears ran down her cheeks. The pain in her chest was squeezing her heart in a death grip. She was thinking of the relief death would bring her if only she could let go. She had never feared life she didn't fear death. Why then was she so stubbornly clinging to a life that had become insulting? She knew the answer: for her granddaughter, for Nati. Her pain lessened, and her breathing eased. Whenever she thought of Nati, the pain became almost tolerable as though the six-year-old girl fought for her grandmother's life. Sometimes she entertained the thought that Nati was an angel looking after her. "God," she whispered, "if you are there anywhere and if you care, watch over my Nati." Again, she remembered Iris's lifeless face, and the bloody bandages floated in front of her eyes. Her breathing became raspy, and she had a coughing fit. On the white sheet that covered her, she saw her own blood.

For three months after Nati's birth, Iris became like a watchdog. She seemed transfigured by motherhood, focused on something outside her for the first time. She didn't let the infant out of her sight. She clung to the baby tenaciously.

Marta tried to reassure her that no one would take Nati away from her, but Iris lived in constant terror. She kept Nati locked with her in the house. At night, the infant slept in her arms. She put ribbons in the baby's hair, made little frocks for her, prepared her food herself because she didn't have milk to nurse. The only person she trusted with Nati was Marta. But when Marta held the baby in her arms, she felt her daughter's eyes sink into her flesh.

Then things changed again.

One Friday evening, when all the members of the kibbutz had gathered in the dining hall to light the Sabbath candles and sing Sabbath songs, she went to Iris's house to see Nati. The house was dark. She opened the door. "Iris!" she called. There was no answer. When she turned on the light, she saw Nati lying on the bed in soiled diapers, whimpering miserably, flailing her tiny fists in the air. Iris was sitting on the bed, staring blankly into the distance.

"Iris?" Marta said softly. Slowly Iris turned to her. Her eyes were dark glass.

"Marta," she said, her voice flat, her face a mask, "I can't."

"I know," Marta said, longing to take her daughter in her arms, to tell her she loved her and that all would be fine. Her arms reached out to Iris then dropped back to her sides. She remembered that Iris couldn't bear being touched. Marta focused her attention on Nati instead, and while she cleaned the baby and changed her diapers, she hummed a song that she used to sing to Iris when she was a baby. Then with Nati in her arms, she turned and said quietly, "I'm taking Nati home with me."

Iris didn't react.

When Ezra came home that night and saw the little girl, he didn't ask any questions. He sat down on the bed and softly caressed Nati's cheek with the back of his index finger. "When she's grown," he said, "I'll take her to the fields with the sheep. It's better than being with people."

"Don't talk nonsense," said Marta. But in her heart of hearts, she wondered if he isn't right.

The next day, she brought Nati to the Children's House. Her one consolation was that Nati would be safe.

After that Friday, Iris rarely left her house. Marta brought Nati to her every evening. Sometimes Iris played with the baby; sometimes she only gazed at her. But as Nati grew, Iris and she became more connected. Iris would tell Nati stories from the Bible or sing to her in gentle voice songs that little girls sing, and on those occasions, affection of a different sort flowed between them. And Nati would sit across from her mother, wishing their time together would last forever. But more often than not, during Nati's visits, Iris would stand silently by the window, staring with glazed eyes at the pecan tree that never gave fruit. Nati would play under the pecan tree close to the house. And while she listened to a noisy chorus of crickets, she would watch the window and hope that her mother would call her, smile at her, be like other mothers were. After a while, she would go back to Marta's house, her head bowed, and her light curls covering most of her little face. Ezra was always waiting for her. He would swipe her in his arms and hoist her up to his shoulders, and she would urge him like urging a horse. "Dio!" she would shout, laughing and crying, embracing his neck tightly with her tiny arms, and he would melt.

Nati was five when Marta became ill. Once she knew that nothing could be done for her at the hospital, she told Dr. Shoham that she wanted to die at home. A few days later, she was back in her own bed.

Iris, who couldn't bear the hospital, would now come every day. She would arrive at three and leave at five. She was never late and never early. She would sit on the straight-backed chair by the shut window, her hands clasped between her knees, her eyes fastened to her mother's in silence.

At first, Marta would talk. She told Iris about her childhood in Poland, about her own mother and how much she had loved her. She told her daughter about her meeting with Ezra at the Zionist camp and how he proposed to her. "Oh, Iris," she smiled, "he was so handsome." And she talked for hours about her early days in Kibbutz Regev. "Those were wondrous days," she said musingly. "We had nothing, we lived in tents we almost drowned in the swamps. Many died of malaria and typhoid fever. But we had a dream. It seemed to us that the God of Moses was right there with us. We were in our glory nothing scared us. Not the scorching sun, not the scarcity of food and water, not even the malaria and typhoid fever, not death itself. We worked and sang and dreamed. Oh yes," she sighed, "We had a dream."

And Iris would sit there in silence, her eyes fastened on Marta's lips; an unexpected serenity softened her face. From time to time, the corners of her lips would quiver, and Marta recalled her daughter's face that time in the hospital, that one time when she had called her mother. Was this a smile or a grimace of pain? She still didn't know. And yet, Iris's silent presence gave Marta a sense of comfort until one day she forgot herself, and the question erupted from her mouth. "Iris, my child, who is Nati's father?"

Iris glared at her, her eyes wild and panic-stricken. Extreme effort was etched on her face, and Marta saw the conflict that erupted in her daughter's mind. Iris's mouth opened and closed, but not a sound came out. Marta waited, her eyes fixed on her daughter's wild eyes. "Iris," she whispered.

Iris stood up. For a long moment, she dug deep into the green eyes fixed upon her; and Marta saw how her daughter's

51

face shut, her body froze, and she was standing there lost—her eyes dark glass. Her heart sinking, Marta saw her daughter vanishing, dissolving in front of her eyes.

For a long time, she lay there looking at the empty chair.

For four days now, Iris hadn't come to visit her.

For four days, the chair remained empty.

"Marta! Marta!" She heard suddenly a voice calling her name, forcing her to surface, not to give up. She opened her eyes. Her friend, Anna, was placing a food tray on a small table beside her bed.

"How do you feel, Marta?" asked Anna, placing a cool hand on the hot, sweat-drenched forehead.

"Have you seen Nati?" Marta asked.

"Yes, she and Little Micha are collecting snails and rainworms by the dining hall."

Anna's eyes were fixed on the red spot on Marta's sheet. She stuffed her hands quickly into her apron pockets and tried not to stare at the bloodstains.

"What's to eat?" Marta tried to say with a light voice.

Anna's face lit up. With a trembling hand, she pushed away a strand of gray hair from her forehead. "As usual," she said, "chicken soup, chicken, and potatoes.

"What else is new?" smiled Marta. But after two spoons of soup, she sighed fatigued. As much as she wished to please Anna, she couldn't eat. She looked at Anna apologetically.

Anna took the food away. "Never mind," she said. "Don't force yourself." After a moment, she asked, "Is Ezra home?"

"Baaaa," bleated Marta weakly.

At that moment, the door burst open. Nati came running in, her face smeared with mud, her eyes excited, full of light. In her hand was an assortment of wildflowers from the field. "For you, Grandma," she laughed and scattered the flowers on Marta's bed then immediately flung open the shutters. "Grandma," she chirped, "I saw three rainbows today, three rainbows, Grandma!

And I collected so many rain worms and snails. Dahlia was mad because we got muddy, and Daphna crushed the worms in her hand, and then she wanted to catch a rainbow and cried when she couldn't. Silly girl! Doesn't she know that you can't catch a rainbow?" Nati gulped a mouthful of air. "Do you know the story of Noah and the ark, Grandma?" She hiccupped. "Mother once told it to me. Oh, Grandma, it was such a wonderful story. All those big animals, lions and elephants and giraffes. But Mother said that Noah took mosquitoes and ants too. I wish she would tell me more stories. Well"—she gulped another breath—"I can ask Grandpa. He knows everything. He told me so. He said he was a teacher, like Dahlia, when he lived in Poland. Grandma, where's Poland?"

"Far," said Marta.

"Very far?"

"Yes, Nati. Very, very far."

"Oh." Nati lifted her eyebrows and crinkled her nose. "Are rainbows because God promised Noah in the Bible never to make a flood anymore? Mother said so."

"Yes, Nati." Marta found a voice inside herself that was free of illness, a confident voice for her granddaughter only.

"Well," said Nati, "if God promised not to make floods anymore, how come Rita's house was flooded yesterday? How come, Grandma? God should keep his promises, shouldn't he, Grandma?" She puckered her lips and waited. But Marta couldn't answer. She felt her lungs and heart being crushed.

"Grandma!" Nati tugged at her hand. "Why didn't God keep his promise? Why did Rita's house flood?" The child picked a flower from the blanket and put it next to Marta's cheek. She placed a marigold in Marta's hand, and Marta inhaled the fragrance of open fields and wet earth. Her fingers fondled the delicate petals of the marigold. Her breathing eased.

"Little Micha said it was a lot of fun to have the house flooded," said Nati. "He bragged that he could swim in the living room. I know that he said that so I would admire him. But it must have been fun. Do you think God might flood our house too?" She shrugged her tiny shoulders. "I hope he does. I hope he doesn't keep his promise. People don't. And anyway, maybe God is sick." She thought for a moment. "God is sick!" She declared, "otherwise, he'd make you well. Mother says God can do everything."

"Maybe he forgot," Marta said.

A pout puckered Nati's face. She said, "Grandpa promised to take me to the fields today, but he forgot—just like God."

"No, Nati. He didn't forget," said Anna. "He didn't want you to get wet and catch a cold. Grandpa loves you very much."

Nati frowned. She looked at Anna then again at Marta. After a moment, she asked Marta, "Didn't you tell Anna that on Saturday you got up from bed and we stood in the rain and I held you by myself and we got wet?"

"No, it's our secret," smiled Marta.

"Oh!" Nati's eyes opened wide. "Our own secret," she said in a conspiratorial voice. "But I thought it's only a secret from Mother."

"Don't worry, Nati," said Marta. "Anna will keep our secret."

Marta closed her eyes. The light in the room was white and harsh and hurt her eyelids like thousands of multicolored needles. "Nati," she said, "please close the door and the shutters."

Nati didn't move from Marta's bed. With her little fist, she rubbed at the mud on her cheek. "There isn't any god!" Nati declared suddenly. She climbed on the narrow bed, cuddled close to Marta, and stuck her thumb in her mouth. Her bright brown curls mingled on the pillow with Marta's gray hair. Marta turned on her side and, for a moment, held the little body to her chest, mysterious warmth flooded her cold body. She closed her eyes and, for a moment, smiled deliciously.

"Grandma."

"Yes, my child?"

"Make me an omelet." Nati didn't remove the thumb from her mouth.

Anna stood up as though in obedience to a command.

"Are you hungry, Nati?" Marta asked.

"Yes," Nati said, "and you make the best omelet in the world. You know, the one with the jam."

"Today, Anna will make your omelet."

Marta's voice was soft and calm, but Anna saw the defeat in her green eyes. Marta's body under the bed cover was hardly visible, a suggestion of a person. Her face was white, but her cheeks glowed red with fever. From time to time, a cough wracked her body. There were several spots of blood on the sheet now.

"No, no, Grandma," Nati insisted. "You can make it. I know you can. Get up, Grandma. Grandma, get up already. Please!"

"Anna," Marta called.

Anna was at her side instantly.

"Help me up," Marta said.

Without a word, Anna helped her out of bed. As she supported her friend, Anna suddenly thought of the clay vase she had inherited from her own mother. The other day, she took it off the shelf intending to dust it, and it crumbled between her fingers.

Now, with great care, Anna held Marta. Nati hovered around them like a bright butterfly anxiously giving orders.

"No, no, Grandma, not that one. The one that Little Micha' Mother made, that one over there, the red one." Anna reached for the strawberry jam; she placed it on the counter in front of Marta. She broke the eggs with one hand while supporting her almost-lifeless friend with the other.

"No," Nati said. "Grandma has to make the omelet. Do it, Grandma!" Her voice was angry, but Marta heard the terror inside the child's body, and the love.

Her fingers felt clumsy and stiff as slowly, silently, she beat the eggs. A heavy fatigue spread through her blood, paralyzing her limbs. For a moment, all her wishes died; and she longed to be in her bed, to sleep for a long time inside the silence, to be one with the void—that behind it there is no guilt, no pain. Her eyelids dropped; her head sank onto her chest. She made a tremendous effort to clear the fog that settled in her brain and accept what was happening to her. She lifted up her head and forced her eyes open, and as she poured the yellow mixture into the pan, she became acutely aware of daffodils and narcissi fragrance wafting in the air. "Ezra," she called silently, "I want Ezra." Then her legs began to shake, and she felt Anna's arms holding her up, almost lifting her off the floor.

"Grandma." Nati pulled at her arm. "You're burning the omelet."

When she turned the omelet with a spatula, she gazed out of the open kitchen window, her eyes filled with wintry brilliance. Odd, she thought, the light seemed less vivid than she knew it to be after rain, as though a fog had moved in. The colors of the trees faded, also the mountains, as though a mist moved in and subdued the light. I know the light is bright and blue, she was thinking, forcing herself to see again the radiance; the light remained muted.

"Almost done. Now the jam." She heard Anna's voice as an echo in her ear. Slowly, silently, Marta spread the jam, while her mind was fastened on the time when she worked in the Children's House, rubbing baby oil on the pure limbs.

Nati squeezed her body between the two women, clasping Marta's waist with her arms and pressing her cheek into her grandmother's back as if she wished to enter into her grandma and give her warmth and life from her own young body.

"I'll hold Grandma," she said, her little arms tightening around Marta.

Suddenly, as though a mysterious hand was at work, the mist lifted, the window brimmed with brilliant light. A sensation of lightness, as if she were nothing but air, came upon her. A scent of fields was thick in her nostrils. She looked at the distant mountains—standing, like hanging between earth and sky, silent and pure, almost white, glimmering in the white light. In her mind's eye, she saw the silvery glint of the leaves on the olive trees in summer. Somewhere a dog barked.

"More jam," said Nati. The child's voice entered Marta's body and stayed there.

"More, more," said Nati.

"It'll burst," Marta said; her eyes wide-open, and she is taking leave of the clouds and the trees and the birds and the mountains. She heard Nati's voice saying into her back, "Let it burst."

"Okay." Marta coughed then whispered, "Nati, you're holding me too tight." Reluctantly, Nati let go of Marta's waist; and slowly, so slowly, Marta turned around. "Here, my child," she said, her voice lifting with pride, "is a king of an omelet." And as she handed Nati the plate with the fat yellow omelet oozing red jam, her hands were as steady as the mountains.

"I knew you could make it, Grandma," Nati said.

"Who said I couldn't?" said Marta.

The room whirled around her. She was falling. Anna caught her, and cradling her like a baby in her strong arms, she carried her back to bed.

From her bed, Marta watched as Nati ate the omelet slowly, licking the last bit of strawberry jam off her fingers without once taking her eyes from Marta's face. Her big, almond shaped brown eyes, like Iris's eyes. When she finished eating, she climbed on Marta's bed, kissed Marta's cracked lips, jumped off, called good-bye to Anna, and ran to the opened door. She halted at the door, turned back to the room, and announced, "I am going to Little Micha's house now. Rita is baking cookies, and she said I can help her." She turned her attention outside. "Oh, look, Grandma, it's raining again."

Marta's lips moved to reply, but Nati was already outside, running toward Little Micha's house.

Anna went to shut the door.

"Leave it open," Marta said.

Anna remained standing at the foot of the bed for a long while.

Marta tried to smile. She spoke no more.

Suddenly she felt a familiar presence, two hands holding hers with strange softness that seeped into her body, enfolding her in a dreamy quiet. "Ezra?" But it was not Ezra. Her eyelids lifted, and her eyes sunk into two huge almond-shaped brown eyes. She saw a wet face, a mouth trembling. Was it a grimace or a smile? She still couldn't tell. "Iris, my child." Her lips moved, but not a word came out. Her eyelids dropped.

"Mother."

She hesitated; then as if through a mist, her hand lifted, and she caressed her daughter's face.

Her hand fell. She floated.

The sun's rays shone in the open door and made Marta's pain turn vague, almost friendly, the room very bright. She saw her mother standing just past the door in the rain, a smile on her face, her arms outstretched. Someone was playing the harmonica, and the bittersweet music of her youth filled the room. Someone is waiting for me, Marta thought. Where is Ezra? But she knew. Ezra was where he belonged, in the green pastures tending the sheep, dreaming of plump women with ripe breasts. Martha smiled, her eyes open.

Outside the rain grew louder.

(A prayer)
Remember with kindness the good
We have done and let us pass
Without unnecessary torture
And without a breathless straining.
Even a bird recognizes that particular place
Remember only the good and breathe
Into us that moment, softly,
Without mocking,
Without unnecessary confusion.

UNTIL DEATH

I shall carry you until death
Erased with life
Every day a little paler.
How long is it going to go on
This eternal torture of the
Vortex of consciousness?
Leave, or close the door
And stay.

In the forest, the shadows perish
Mist devours the trees
I will knit for you a dress of lilies.
I understand,
Now rest
Before
you
cross.

LOVE WAVES TO ME

Love waves to me from afar
for I couldn't touch her from near
perhaps I will try to give her birth
let the dream shatter in the mirror of reality
and let reality be caught in the mirror of the dream
let my voice reach you from distances.
But how will my voice cross
the deserts of distances
between man and man
who is chained to his needs
worships his image

*

And time cries the
silence of its shapes
it has no time to erupt
with each pain.

*

And how should I tell in details
and say today was a day
morning sun and night
and the dreams in my sleep
a battle of existence—

*

I wished to build a path in the air
but the air rejected my way
so I quarried for myself a mysterious place
between the sheets
and if he commands me
and raise a big row
I say,
my love, think of me as dead.

*

In my hair I weave eternal flowers
I suck the honey from hell
my flowers are droopy summer and winters
my pleasures corruption and doom.
At night I inhale from the grass of delight
bitter smoke to calm the dark:

dance of nirvana
seduction of Madonna
a saint nailed
to a rotten wood

And with a dry mouth
a dumb smirk of a fish
I smear a blind smile
on the moon.

*

In the sphere of sorrow
and memories
flowers devour the senses
and the heart split wide
torn by shards of
the Milky Way that bursts
in nights of pain and love—
an arrow shot
into the soul of
a nonexistent god.
But the nightingale
forever sings
bleeds,
hangs doomed
on the rosebush
his heart pierced
by a delicate
thorn.

*

These tiny sparks
fondling all that
remained solid
all that didn't yet decay
in this land that
cries blood on its
desecrated mezuzahs
and only these tiny sparks
quiver for a moment—

*

Each day the light turns
the color of man's blood
and above
angels play
with the world's rusty wheel
that with a shout
rolls among borders
repelled in a holocaust of man
forever
man will not rest
for death he brings on himself
and forever longs
for revenge
and he rises up on himself
with drowned sword
to sever his veins
while he screams
his
longing
for
love.

THE KISSING STONE

(ALYA)

And when the silence was at its deepest, the stillness so complete and undisturbed that even the crickets ceased their shouting, and the guard on duty was dozing off somewhere. Alya arose from her bed as if obeying a command and, dressed in her nightclothes, went to the door and opened it. For a long moment, she stood at the open door listening, then closed the door behind her and walked into the night. The way she walked was more like floating, down the moonlit path, straight toward the old water tower where a month earlier, wrapped in bloodstained army blankets, five corpses had lain on the ground; five dead soldiers.

She sang softly, *"I am dreaming, and my eyes can see . . . Anemones, red, red anemones . . ."*

Time leaped back. Again she saw them, lying in a straight line, their naked feet sticking out of the bloody blankets. She bent down and, one after the other, lifted the blankets and searched the faces and with the tips of her fingers, touched the faces. But he wasn't among them. "Gill!" she called. "Gill!"

And began walking around the dead soldiers just as she had walked then—that day, during the war, the day they'd brought the bodies. *"Red, red anemones,"* she sang until she heard Gill's voice, and his voice was soft, clear, and bright.

"Tomorrow will be a beautiful day. Go to the woods. To our secret place."

"Yes," she said. "Yes, tomorrow, in the woods, our secret places. Yes. Listen, Gill, I've something important to tell you . . ." But Gill was gone, the dead soldiers vanished; she alone was standing by the old water tower, smiling at nothing. And still singing Gill's favorite tune, she returned to her room. She went on singing, even softer, as she got back into her bed. For a while, she lay quietly, her eyes wide-open; and she remembered the sky that seemed almost black, each star a burning flame, the moon bigger and brighter than she ever saw it, the moss that sprouted out of the cracks in the cement of the old water tower, the smell of death on the soldiers' faces as she leaned close to touch them. Then the night around her softened, and only Gill's gentle voice lingered in her mind, lulling her into sleep.

And while Alya slept a dreamless sleep, in another bed in the same room, Orna pulled the covers over her head, her brain alert and restless though her body lay rigid and still. The fear she came face-to-face with every night when Alya left the room did not end when Alya returned; and in order to bring sleep, Orna closed her eyes, longing to dive into the realm of dreams, to evolve toward more satisfying form of existence. And she fastened her mind on the happy memories of her childhood, before the war.

And while Alya slept and Orna conjured up pictures of happy, carefree days, in the bed under the window, Ruthie turned toward the wall, beset by ominous thoughts: How long was this lunacy going to go on? Weren't they going to do something about Alya? The war was over. Why don't they do something? Tears of frustration wet her pillow as she lay there in the suffocating stillness, waiting to sleep.

On Saturday afternoon, Orna was sitting on the lawn in a spot of brilliant sunlight, lost in gloomy thoughts, as she leafed abstractedly through a small book of poetry. Her head ached, her temple throbbed, and her eyelids were sore and slightly puffy after a night of troubled sleep. She let the book drop to the grass, closed her eyes, and abandoned herself to the consoling warmth of the afternoon sun. Her face relaxed a little. From one of the houses, she heard faint singing. *"Red, red anemones . . ."*

She sat motionless while the song lasted. When it stopped, she opened her eyes and raised her head. Suddenly she noticed Alya slinking like a tomcat between trees and shrubberies, careful to avoid meeting anyone.

Perhaps Orna knew what her friend was up to. Perhaps she didn't. But she leaped to her feet and called, "Alya!" And she watched as her friend halted abruptly, then turned and slowly came across the grass toward her.

"Well," Orna said, "why are you sneaking around like a criminal?"

"I am going to the woods," said Alya.

Orna felt her heart lurch in her chest. "You can't be serious," she said in a fierce whisper, fixing her blue eyes wide-open upon Alya.

"Why not? I love the woods."

Orna, striving to keep her voice even, said, "I love the woods too. But I don't go there."

Alya smiled enigmatically. "That's because you don't have a soul."

"What do you mean I don't have a soul? Oh, never mind, you and your fancy words." Orna leaned forward, her face almost touching Alya's. "Tell me," she breathed. "You might as well tell me because I saw you talking to him. Alone." Orna felt like punching Alya—actually, all day she felt like punching someone, anyone.

"I'm meeting Ari in the woods at five o'clock," said Alya.

Orna lost her cool altogether. "Are you mad? You don't even know him."

"I know him," said Alya. "He's nice. He's a poet."

"So? He's old. I hear he's twenty and maybe even more." Orna, feeling helplessly annoyed, glared at her friend. "What's wrong with you anyway? Don't you ever read the paper?"

"Orna, you're in love with him." Alya's voice was low and even.

"I'm not." Orna made a desperate effort to sound nonchalant.

"Oh," muttered Alya.

"Oh what?" Orna barked at her friend.

"I'm glad you're not in love with him. That's all," said Alya, her voice slightly apologetic.

Orna stared at her friend, her blue eyes wild. No, she concluded to herself she's definitely nothing special to look at. She looks ten, not fifteen, and she doesn't even have boobs. She's so skinny. Orna took a deep breath, deliberately extending her well-developed breasts. Thank God I don't have freckles and red hair, she thought and, with a flick of her head, tossed her long yellow hair then noticed that Alya's eyes were fixed upon her face with a sort of an innocent yet mischievous glint, and that her lips parted slightly in a little smile. Yes, Orna thought, it's this innocent look in her eyes, this smile. She recalled Ruthie telling her the other day that people were talking about how strange Alya has become.

"The last rumor," Ruthie had said with a weird look of excitement on her plump baby face, "is that at night, Alya has been seen walking near that awful place by the old water tower where the dead soldiers had lain, talking and singing and calling her father's name. And I heard people say if this continues, something drastic should be done."

Orna, determined in her loyalty to Alya, immediately jumped to her friend's defense. "This is a vicious rumor. Alya sleeps in the same room with you and me, and I've never seen her leave in the middle of the night or talk to herself. And as far as calling out her father's name—honestly, Ruthie, sometimes you make me sick. Don't you understand anything?"

"You know it's true," Ruthie had said. "Every night you wait for her to return from the old water tower. Every night. And even after she returns, you can't sleep, and neither can I. So don't pretend you don't know."

Yes, of course, Orna knew. Everyone knew.

Now, looking at Alya's upturned face, Orna thought how changed Alya was by her father's death. Not that she was ever ordinary; everything about her was a little eccentric, out of accord with the rest of her friends. But as time passed, it has become more and more apparent that Alya no longer inhabited their world, that she lived in a private world of her own where all dimension had seemed to be eliminated between the living and the dead, a mysterious world that belongs only to her and Gill. And when people mentioned the war or talked of death, a hard and remote expression would invade Alya's face, leaving her brilliant brown eyes expressionless. And she would walk way. And Orna would watch her with anxious heart, a tide of pain rising to her chest, and she would follow her friend, walk by her side, and silently watch Alya's pale, almost luminous, face. And she would swallow her tears.

And of course, everyone talked about the war—that was all they have been talking about. So more often than not, instead of going to school, Alya would go to the woods of the olive grove, sit under a tree, and read, mostly dream. And sometimes Orna would find her fast asleep with her face buried in a bunch of yellow dandelions that grew in abundance under the trees. Alya would say that school was boring, that she was so happy in the woods and the grove. "Don't tell on me, Orna. Please don't tell on me," she would plead. So, if anyone asked her if she knew where Alya was, Orna would merely shrug her shoulder and say impatiently, "What am I, her keeper? How should I know?" And yet, Alya's growing remoteness was very difficult for Orna to bear.

And now Alya was going to the woods to meet this stranger, Ari, the new poetry teacher. "Alya," Orna said, sadness mingled with impatience replacing her anger, "don't you know it's dangerous to go to the woods?"

"Dangerous? Why?"

"Why? Why do you think there are still so many soldiers there? And what about the mines? Don't you remember when Boaz stepped on a mine and everyone in the kibbutz was sure he would die?"

"Gill had said Boaz wouldn't die." Alya smiled serenely. "Gill knows everything."

Orna wanted to scream that Gill was dead, that he was killed in the war and would never come back. But she merely looked at the ground and viciously kicked at the grass with the toe of her shoe.

"You have a morbid mind, Orna," Alya said. "You make up all kinds of stories. You see demons and evil spirits everywhere—you scare yourself crazy. And you're always confusing things. It's true that Boaz stepped on a mine, but it didn't happen in the woods, it happened near the cornfield. And the papers, I don't read the papers. And besides, Ari will be there to protect me.

"How? Does he have a gun?" Orna was rapidly losing her temper again.

But Alya merely smiled. "No," she said. "He doesn't have a gun. He has a book of poetry."

Orna leaned forward a little and, glaring straight into Alya's eyes, said, "He's so odd and so silent, you shouldn't be alone with him. Did you see the scar on his cheek? Ruthie told me that during the war, he was with the commando unit in the Arava desert and got wounded in the face by shrapnel. Ruthie also said that he never talks about the war because he saw terrible things happen there, and that—for three months after he got wounded—he didn't talk at all, and that he himself almost got killed, and—" Orna clamped a hand over her mouth, letting out a low sound, as she saw the familiar empty look in Alya's eyes; and as her friend turned away from her, she grabbed her hand. "Alya," she groaned, "I'm sorry."

Alya turned back to face her friend. She stood silent, her face remote, her eyes turned inward. "I have to go now," she said after a moment and walked away.

"Alya! Wait!" Orna called, sobbing.

Alya walked toward the gate of the kibbutz. Her dog Amos trotted at her side, licking her hand. His damp black eyes were begging for her attention, but his efforts were not being paid as usual. "Go home, Amos," Alya said. The dog fixed accusing, hurt eyes on her and whined mournfully. Then he laid back his ears, turned around, and crouched at the kibbutz gate to wait.

Outside the gate of the kibbutz, Alya began to run. It was two miles from the kibbutz to the woods, and the world around her glistened green and pure and tranquil. The old eucalyptuses on each side of the road rushed by her as if moving backward. She ran fast, trying not to think. But it was no use. She couldn't stop the incessant chatter of her mind. She was remembering how, when after poetry class on Friday, Ari had stopped her and asked if she could meet him somewhere—anywhere, she should only name the place—on Saturday at five. He took her by such surprise that for a moment she merely stood gaping at him then flushed, her mind twisting with confusion. "Why me?" But he said with an encouraging smile, "To read poetry." She looked at him closely and noticed two bitter-looking lines around his mouth. His hair was black and curly, his face narrow and dark, and his lips full. A red scar in the shape of a rose was etched high on his right cheekbone. But it was his eyes that touched her imagination: deep-set black eyes that looked at her with gentleness and appreciation. Perhaps the way Gill's eyes looked at her. I like him, she thought.

"To read poetry?" She paused. "Okay."

"Where should we meet?"

"Go to the woods. To our regular place," says Gill.

"In the woods," came out of her mouth like in a dream. "By the Kissing Stone."

"The Kissing Stone?"

She blushed, giggled nervously, and bit her lips. "It's only a name of a big white rock in the woods."

He said nothing, only looked at her with his head tilted. "Well," she said with a sort of daring shyness, "it's only a rock. When our parents lived inside the woods, they named it the Kissing Stone."

"I didn't know the kibbutz was built inside the woods."

"There are many things about us you don't know."

He laughed. "But I'm learning fast. Why did they move from the woods to the hill?"

"They had to. Living in the woods wasn't safe then because—oh, I don't remember that time, I was only a little girl. Anyway, the Kissing Stone is easy to sit on, and you can't miss it because it's the biggest rock in the woods, and it's very, very white."

She looked around, unsure of being seen with him alone. People talk. *Oh never mind,* she thought. *Let them talk they would anyhow.* And when he said, "I hear the woods isn't exactly a safe place now either," she pulled herself up and looked defiantly into his eye, challenging. "It's safe enough," she said. "I go there all the time." Then a small devil leaped inside her, and a little mischievous smile lifted the corners of her mouth. She said, "Except of course for the snakes." She saw the look in his eyes change.

"Big snakes?" he asked, his voice hushed but subtle, stroking her nerves like a balm.

She whispered, "Enormous," and watching him laugh, she laughed with him. But the moment was a difficult one for her—perhaps for him too.

Now, recalling the entire scene, each detail fresh and alive. Alya felt hot and sticky. Not quite real. And he had chosen her, and she wondered how a thing like that could have happened to her. If I were he, she was thinking, I would have chosen Orna. Orna is so sophisticated, adventurous, and of course, the prettiest.

My beautiful girl, my clever little honeybee, says Gill.

Near the woods, Alya slackened her pace. Her legs felt strange as though her knees were made of gum. Her red hair stuck to her flushed, damp cheeks, and her shirt was soaking wet.

Is that what Gill means when he talks about love? She wondered. At that moment, she wished Amos, her dog, was with her, or even Orna.

"Oh, don't panic. It'll be all right," she admonished herself.

When she reached the edge of the woods, she stopped running and stood listening. She listened not only with her ears but also with her whole being, her face assuming an odd, mystical expression. After a moment, she took off her shoes and slowly entered the woods. The stillness was complete and soothing, stroking her nerves like a mother's gentle hand. The damp pine needles yielded submissive and soft under the light pressure of her bare feet, and red winter sun acting as a chaperone winked at her through the branches of the trees. The ground was crimson with anemones. She sang softly, *"Red, red anemones . . ."*

She picked an anemone and slightly caressed her face with its delicate petal, inhaling the fresh and poignant fragrance of recent rain and pine needles. She walked slowly, feeling the warmth of the sun on her back and shoulders, when suddenly the stillness was interrupted by a loud, abrupt metallic sound. She turned quickly but saw nothing unusual, only dense blanket of scarlet, white, and yellow flowers beneath the tall grass and under the trees. The wild thumping of her heart subsided. She sighed and shrugged then, singing, entered the long, narrow path of the cypresses. After a while, she turned to the right where the pine branches entwined, converging into an awning, shading her head. With the anemone's flowers, she wove a red laurel with which she adorned her head and forehead, securing it with hairpins. A slight breeze began to stir. She saw the tops of the cypresses sway gently. Sparrows and wagtails and bulbuls and red-breasted robins sang all around her. Then she saw the Kissing Stone, solid as ever. And there was Ari, sitting on its flat surface, reading from a small book.

Dazed with excitement, Alya became almost unconscious of her surroundings, a little frightened. Holding her breath, she crept closer and watched him from behind the thick gnarled trunk of an old acacia tree. She thought him beautiful. Suddenly he got up and began to recite. She couldn't hear the words he uttered; his voice was only a murmur. But his face was entirely visible to her, and she saw him grimace and gesture wildly like a mad actor on an invisible stage. She giggled. He looked around. "Alya?" She crouched lower behind the tree's trunk. She saw him look at his watch. She looked at hers. Five o'clock. She stood still, listening again, completely absorbed.

"Here I come," she said, and from among the shadows of the trees, she stepped out into the bright light of the clearing. With the red laurel on her head, she walked bravely to meet him.

He turned and saw her standing with her shoes in her hand, her feet bare and mud caked, and the red anemones laurel circling her head like little leaping flames. He gazed at her, enchanted, his face white and tense, his right hand clutching the book of poetry to his chest. She looked so young and timid it scared him, made him feel uncertain in himself. The reality of their situation suddenly confused him. What were his intentions toward her?

From the moment he had seen her she dominated his thoughts. He wished to be alone with her, to know her. And yet, as much as he was attracted to her, something about her disturbed him, made him feel perplexed. She was completely different from anyone he'd ever met. She seemed always to be mocking a little. Not overtly, not obvious, and definitely without malice; but it was there in the glint of her eyes, in her smile. Her smile—the most charming smile he had ever seen on a human face yet also most disquieting. A smile that was ironic and sweet, innocent yet knowing, pure joy and passion mixed with deep sorrow. And still he felt compelled to know her.

"Alya, you're really here," he said softly, trying to hide his confusion.

"Yes," she laughed.

Not knowing what else to say, he asked, "Did you see the soldiers?"

"No," she said, and he saw her body stiffen. He looked at her in wonder.

She liked his shyness. It made him seem younger, and it made her feel older, a little bolder. But she wasn't going to talk about wars or death, and she hoped he wasn't going to talk about it either. She wouldn't be able to bear it. She would have to walk away from him, and she didn't want to walk away from him.

I like him, she thought. His eyes are so gentle.

She stood meditating and looked deep into the shade of the dense foliage, listening to the songs of the insects in the grass. She was conscious of his eyes upon her and his silence. She hesitated a moment then, with a small frown on her face, said, "The woods seem somehow different."

"Different?" he asked. "How?"

"The woods seem so calm today as if hiding an important secret. Orna would say, 'It is full of demons and spirits.' She giggled, embarrassed at her own words.

"Probably because of the soldiers," he said. "They seem to be everywhere."

She said nothing but looked at him so intently, her face pale, her eyes pained. Suddenly she felt trapped in her loneliness, lost inside herself, and as if she were cold, she hugged her shoulders.

Only a bad dream Shhh . . . says Its Gill.

Perhaps at that moment, as she met his eyes, and he saw the terrible pain in them, Ari began to understand, to know her. He reached out his hand as if to wipe off the fear from her heart. She looked at him, transfixed. His fingers touched her cheek. She shut her eyes. She felt as if she wanted to hide herself in him, in his gentleness, in his strength. She opened her eyes.

Shhh . . . don't be afraid of. I'm here, says Gill.

She sat on the stone's surface, her head turned toward the setting sun, her eyes squinting at the early-evening radiance. For a while they sat in silence—she looking at the sky, he looking at her. Then she turned to him and said, "This stone means so much to so many," and with the open palm of her right hand, she slowly, sensually caressed the stone. Perhaps she was thinking about his hand on her face.

"Tell me about it." He took her hands and held them for a moment between his.

"It means happiness and disappointments, dreams and love and—death. When our parents were young, they used to meet here." She blushed. "Oh," she said in a little voice, "I don't really know how to talk about it. It's our parents' secret." And suddenly she felt foolish, sitting like that in the exposed clearing with the red anemones laurel on her head and her hands held in his. But her hands felt right and comfortable in his. Perhaps more. The blush deepened on her cheeks.

"Let's read poetry," Ari said. He jumped off the stone, pulling her with him, spread a blanket on the grass, and sat upon it. She sat next to him, her shoulder barely touching his. She removed the hairpins from the red laurel and let it slide down around her neck. As she leaned back against the Kissing Stone, her fear disappeared. She felt safe with him. He opened his book of poetry and read to her simply, his voice rich. She closed her eyes and tipped her head back until it rested on the stone, listening to the poet's words and the man's voice. At that moment, she felt in harmony with the red sun and the tranquil universe.

And when you're completely silent, you'll hear the wings of the butterflies, says Gill.

Ari closed the book and quietly looked at her.

"How beautiful." She smiled. "Poetry. Gill loves poetry."

"Gill?" He looked at her questioningly.

For a moment, she looked at him in silence, as if not sure that she wants to tell him. "Gill is my father," she said in a quiet, soft vice. "The people in the kibbutz say he was killed in the war by a bullet. But to me he's alive. He's always with me. He talks to me. People think I'm mad, and perhaps they are right, but I have no choice. You'd like Gill. You're like him, a little. Would you like to know him?"

"Yes," Ari said.

Slowly she withdrew her hands from his. She sat completely still with only a smile on her lips; and her brown eyes, full of light and shadows, gazed at the sky with a sort of rapture. Perhaps she was hearing Gill's voice at that moment.

She spoke very softly: "Gill and I come here every day in winter. Gill talks to me about the butterflies and the birds and the flowers and trees and of all the earth's creatures. Gill and I, we have a bond between us. Gill never says, 'Go to school, Alya. You've got to be like everyone else, Alya.' He says, 'Come, the vineyards are heavy with grapes, the orchards laden with fruit. Come let us go for a heavenly walk.' That's the way Gill

[handwritten marginalia: Why not Mum & Dad? Do children get divorced parents in Israel?]

talks. And we walk in the fall and in winter, and we walk in the spring and in summer. And we walk for hours. And Gill always hums a tune to himself, and his voice is joyful, his eyes are full of light and always laughing. Gill's eyes are green, and his hair is red, thick, and curly like lamb's wool. When Rina, my mother, wants to tease him, she says he looks like a broom caught on fire, but to me he looks like a pillar of light.

"Sometimes Rina would join us on our walks but not very often because she isn't very strong. She is delicate and tires quickly. But then Rina doesn't care for the vineyards and orchards and woods the way Gill and I do. She says it's awfully hot there and sticky, and there are millions of bees and wasps and all kinds of dangerous creatures living among the grapes, peaches, apples, and flowers. Once, in the vineyard, a wasp stung me, my face was swollen for days, and my eyes disappeared altogether. I looked so ugly just like I did when I had the mumps. Gill called me a chipmunk and said it wasn't so bad; it'll toughen me up. But Rina was terribly upset and fussed over me as if I were critical. I loved being fussed over like that by Rina. Gill kept teasing her and quoting to her from the Bible, saying that like the *Shulamit, she was fairest among women, and he called her his lily of the valley.* And he took her in his arms and kissed her until she stopped talking, and I saw her burrow her face in his woolly coarse red hair, and in his hair, she later told me, she smelled the fields and the earth and the air. And he made her forget all that existed outside of themselves, and that was very nice and made me very happy. Rina and Gill are crazy about each other, and Gill once told me that he kissed Rina for the first time right here on the Kissing Stone. Rina says that Gill and I are birds of a feather, and that we'll be the death of her, we're so wild. I wish Rina could feel him like I do. But she doesn't. And she has that funny look on her face when I say that he is only lost somewhere, and she has to find him. Then it won't hurt so much, and she won't feel so lonely. She looks at me, a strange smile appears on her face, and I can tell that she doesn't see me at all. Perhaps she sees Gill. I don't really know. And she begins to cry, silently pulls me to her, and kisses me all over my face, and her tears wet my face, and she moans and sighs so sadly I want to run away. It's unbearable."

Alya looked at Ari. "Have you ever met her?"

Ari didn't answer. He was sitting erect, his body utterly still as though held by a terrible tension; and his face, she saw, was suddenly distorted as if he were gripped by an intolerable pain.

Ari wiped the sweat from his brow. Someone, or was it something, was laughing at him with a piercing shriek. Shells whistled around him. The jeep he was driving blew right from under him. Three of his friends were torn to pieces. He pressed his open palm to the wound in Dan's throat. He was drenched in Dan's blood; the taste of it was in his mouth. He was breathing blood; blood was on his face, on his hands, in his eyes. "Dan!" he screamed. "Dan! Don't die!" But Dan, his best friend, was dead. He stopped breathing just like that. The terrible rage of that moment threatened once more to obliterate his sanity. He felt the nausea rising up in him. The ghastly, helpless feeling was with him. In him. He was in agony and was unable, for a moment, to collect himself.

His mind was still locked on the image of his dying friend when he felt a pressure on his hand. And when he turned his head and looked at her, he was looking out of his chaos down into her uplifted, faintly flushed face and vivid brown eyes.

"Gill says pain is only an illusion," Alya said. "And Gill once told me that the Bushmen of the Kalahari Desert say there is a dream always dreaming us." Then she smiled and removed the red anemones laurel from around her neck, and crouching on her knees, she slowly placed it at the edge of the blanket. "For Gill." She hesitated a moment, then turned her head and looked at him. "You understand, don't you? About Gill, I mean."

Yes, he knew. He understood. She lived inside her imagination. She was chained to the ghost of her dead father as he was chained to the ghost of his slain friend. And for one breathless moment, he imagined himself setting her free, bearing her away. Suddenly he saw the man, Gill, shot through the chest, lying on the arid ground of the Arava desert with the hot wind roughing his flame-like hair, his eyes open into a blue and empty heaven.

Ari clenched his fists.

And as if reading his thoughts, he heard her whisper, "If I let go of Gill now, I'll lose him forever."

"Yes," he said.

They looked at each other. He took her hand again. They sat in silence and listened to their ghosts as they watched the winter sun bleeding its dying rays over the branches of the trees.

The moment Alya disappeared from her sight; Orna went quickly to the room she shared with her and Ruthie. She put on an old pair of sneakers and a white sweater over her blouse and tied a scarf around her blond curls. Suddenly she sat down on her bed and stared in front of her as if in a spell, her heart boiling with raging and conflicting emotions. Of course, she was jealous of Ari being sweet on Alya and not on her, but she also knew that wasn't what made her feel so utterly devastated. She couldn't understand the restlessness that came upon her with such a force. She felt bewildered, afraid, and unbearably sad. "Oh," she cried and banged her fists on the bed. "One day, I'll go away. Away from hate, from wars, from death." She kept hitting the bed with her clenched fist until her hands were raw. She felt no relief. She thought of another conversation she had with Ruthie: Ruthie had said, "This Alya, she's always up to something weird like going to the woods where no one goes now. And the way she talks about her father. Real freaky. She seems to be the only one in the kibbutz who doesn't know that he's dead. And the way she never cries. Never. She didn't cry the day they told her that he was dead, she didn't shed a tear at his funeral. Not a tear. You saw how she was. You stood at her side as they lowered him into the ground. You never took your eyes from her, and you didn't cry either. I must say, Orna, you looked almost as crazy as she did. She. Standing there like a stranger looking at the sky. Smiling. I thought I'd die. My god, Orna, she's mad. Really crazy."

"Shut up," Orna hissed. "Just shut up."

Recalling that conversation, Orna suddenly felt, as she had felt many times and especially since Gill's death, that she had to protect Alya against herself. I should have found a way to prevent her from going to the woods. *How could I have been so blinded by jealousy? How? How?* And then finally came the tears. Tears that had choked her throat that entire day, that entire year. At that moment, like many she had experienced during the war, the world seemed to her dim and grim and menacing—full of evil, infested with demons. "I must go to the woods," she cried. "I must go to the woods now!" And with her eyes still full of tears, she ran out the door and toward the gate of the kibbutz, where Amos, Alya's dog, was still whining but again to no avail. Ignoring the dog, Orna studied the gate for a moment then turned around. She decided to go through the olive grove. It was a bit faster to reach the woods from there, but the ground was still muddy from recent rain, and her feet sunk into the wet earth, slowing her pace. Above her, the olive trees stretched their bare branches, motionless, like dark arms. She could still hear the dog's mournful whine, and trying to suppress a feeling of a sudden dread, she began to whistle and hastened her pace until she reached the old acacia trunk where she crouched to observe.

Leaning against the Kissing Stone, bathed in the last glow of the red evening light, they looked like images in a dream. Alya was talking, and Ari was listening. The red anemones laurel was around Alya's neck, and her mouth was curved in an enchanted smile. Orna knew well that look of rapture on her friend's face. "Oh no," Orna whispered. "Don't talk about Gill. Please, please, Alya, don't talk about Gill." Would she ever be able to let him go? Would things ever be the way they used to be?

"Is my happy childhood over?" Orna asked herself in a whisper.

"Yes, it's really over," she answered herself with bitter finality. Her depression, her suffering, time alone would be the healer. Time. She wondered.

When she saw Alya remove the anemones laurel from around her neck and place it, with so much reverence, at the edge of the blanket, Orna understood the significance behind that gesture. She sang softly in a halting, broken voice, *"Red, red anemones . . ."*

Behind the top of the trees, the red sun lolled westward. The dusk deepened. Only a trace of twilight lingered in the sky. Rain clouds were gathering; the tops of the cypresses waved restlessly. As the night advanced, it grew cold. Orna shivered. She felt cramped in her hiding place. Slowly she began to rise when somewhere nearby she heard a branch of a tree snap suddenly. She crouched back. Did I hear footsteps? Someone breathing? Must be one of the soldiers. She waited. Nothing. Only the breeze playing, moving through the treetops, scuffing the grass, and birds calling out as they settled for the night.

How dumb of me to be so jumpy. I should watch out for my own wild imagination. She leaned her face against the rough bark of the old acacia and gazed into the long shadows of the woods. Suddenly she went rigid. Two flickering black eyes were staring into hers with grisly grin of malice.

Orna screamed. She leaped up. Her face distorted with terror, she ran toward the Kissing Stone. Ari caught her as she stumbled and almost fell. She clung to him, howling and babbling incoherently. She heard Alya's urgent voice. "Orna! What are you doing here? What is it?"

Orna let go of Ari and looked at Alya with horror-stricken eyes. "There"—she pointed to the old acacia, her teeth chattering—"I . . . I saw something evil . . . A man . . . A demon with murder in his eyes . . . There . . . there . . . I saw the devil. There is danger in the woods. Terrible danger. Let's get out of here before we're dead."

Alya took her friend's hands. She said, "Orna, Orna, no one is there. See, Ari is looking behind the acacia tree. Look, he's coming back. All you saw were the shadows of trees and flowers and animals. Calm down. Calm down."

Orna released her breath, but the horror lingered in her eyes. "This place gives me the creeps, it's so spooky. I am sure I saw something." And leaning her trembling arms on the Kissing Stone, she hid her face in her hands. "Alya,'" she sobbed, "I was so jealous, and then suddenly, I had the feeling that something awful is going to happen to you. Really. I'm so ashamed for the lunatic way I've behaved." She looked at Ari. His face was very pale and very silent, but she saw no surprise on his face, no confusion. She tried to smile.

Ari put his hand on her shaking shoulder. "Don't cry, Orna. It's all right now. You had a bad fright. It's really all right." He turned to Alya. "It will be completely dark soon. Let's go back."

But looking beyond them, far into the woods, Alya saw a soldier approaching. "Look," Alya cried and pointed. "It's only a soldier after all. Only a soldier," she whispered to herself faintly.

Orna wheeled around, and still crying and at the same time laughing hysterically, she waved her arms frantically.

"Let's go," Ari said. "Now!" He was looking in the direction of the old acacia. His face tightened with sudden tension. But Alya didn't seem to see or hear him. She merely stood and listened to the woods.

The soldier raised both arms and waved back; and as he ran toward them, his machine gun swung at his side, its metal glittering red in the fading twilight.

"What's going on? What are you doing in the woods?" The soldier's voice was low and angry.

"We're going back," Ari said.

"Then hurry."

A look passed between the soldier and Ari. The soldier made a signal with his head in the direction of the old acacia, and Ari acknowledged it with a slight nod of his head. He grabbed Alya by the hand. "Come on. Let's go. Quick." She was startled by the sudden sharpness of his voice but went with him without resisting.

The soldier grabbed Orna's arm. "I'll walk with you to the edge of the woods," he said in the same low, angry voice.

"Let go. You're hurting me." Orna tried to free her arm. The soldier ignored her and walked with rapid, almost-running strides, pulling her roughly.

They were only a short distance from the Kissing Stone when the shooting began. The soldier cursed. "Run!" he cried and pushed Orna toward Ari and Alya. She stumbled. Ari caught her by the hand. They saw the soldier swing around and fire in the direction of the old acacia.

They saw him fall. They heard him hit the ground.

"Get down behind the Kissing Stone!" Ari shouted. They ran back amidst a spray of bullets ricocheting,—whistling all around them, lodging in the barks of trees, bouncing off rocks, hitting the ground. Shots exploded everywhere. Shots and shouts. Hell.

Alya stopped running and stood rooted to the earth. Her face was lifted; and her eyes were staring, far into the darkening sky above her head.

Still running, Orna turned her head. She screamed, "Alya! Get down!"

But Alya didn't move.

"Oh my god! Alya!" Orna almost reached her friend when a bullet struck her between her shoulder blades. She leaped forward and hit the Kissing Stone. Three more bullets entered her body, painting her white sweater dark purple. On the flat surface of the stone, she lay facing the sky, her blue eyes wide-open. And her face was that of the child she so yearned to be.

Ari stumbled. His body struck the moist ground. With his fingernails, he clawed the earth and, with his last breath, dragged himself to where Alya lay. He collapsed at her side, his head barely touching her right shoulder. He felt his head burning, blood blinding his eyes.

To touch her face. Can't move. Can't see. It's so dark. The clamor in his head was unbearable. He vomited. Then relief. No pain. Silence. *Dan? Dan?*

At the foot of the Kissing Stone, Alya was lying on her back, her fingers moving, caressing the grass. With feverish eyes, she watched the fog descend over the tops of the trees slowly, enveloping the universe with a halo of light. And through the light, a voice called: *come let us go for a heavenly walk.*

She lost consciousness.

After a while, she awoke dizzy with pain. What's happening? Where was she hit? Was this blood? Was it really the end? What was this smell in the air? Rain? Was it rain on her face? She tried to move her legs. Impossible. Her hand groped around. Her fingers touched Ari's head. She summoned all her willpower and lifted herself up, supporting her body on her left elbow. She looked down at his inert face. "Ari," she whispered, "Ari." His eyes were staring at the sky. With her right hand, she touched his cheeks. His face was still warm, his flesh still firm. Was it blood on her hand?

Now. So easy to break the cord of life. Now. A little push. A last breath. A mere glide from here to there.

85

She collapsed. The silence and darkness were heavy around her. She was sinking fast. Suddenly, behind her closed eyelids, a blast of light. She opened her eyes. Lightning. The air was flushed with lightning, the sky white.

I want to live. I want to live, her mind screamed. "Orna!" she called. "Orna!"

Somewhere in the woods, a night bird screamed.

She pushed herself up again. She turned her head. She saw Orna lying on the Kissing Stone, the growing darkness, shrouding her body layer by layer like gauze. Her face, illuminated by the lightning, she looked ghostly.

Orna. Orna.

Alya lost her courage. She lay there mad with pain. *To sleep. Not to know. So much fear. Gill. Gill.*

Don't be afraid. I'm here. It's only a bad dream. Here. That's better. Nothing bad will happen to my little girl. Shhh. Tomorrow will be a beautiful day, says Gill.

Suddenly she smiled, and in a clear voice she said, "Good-bye, Gill."

She closed her eyes.

Ari. Orna. Gill. Orna. Orna. Orna. Don't tell on me, Orna. Please don't tell on me.

She heard voices. Familiar voices. A dog bark.

I can't. Hurry. Hurry.

She fainted and awoke and again fainted. After some time, when her own screams pulled her back from the night into semiconscious numbness of cold and pain, she saw, like in a dream, the wind torches coming near. She heard voices and barks. She felt the hands lifting her up. Faces swayed above her, blurred masks. Something warm and wet on her face. A dog whined.

And the last thing she was aware of before she sank back into the dark was the fragrance of the rain, the pines, and the wet earth.

UNICORN

Do not let them take me,
You, my unicorn.
I have a thousand faces you know them all,
You created them in darkness.
Why did you dream me lacking, tiny, severed?
Touch me with your horn.
I am tired of climbing mountains,
Lie with me among the flowers.
You said when I enter the garden, the unicorn
Will welcome me, and I a field of poison ivy entered.
I shall heal myself with sweet herbs, with quiet waters.
I shall come to you new, fragrant, flowing.

MANNEQUIN

That day I was a mannequin:
my head and torso hanging from a beam
my limbs scattered on the floor
my face tinted the color of despair
my eyes empty wounds
void of color or lashes
regarding the world without
death or consciousness.
And although the experts knew
I was merely a mannequin
they were careful not to touch
me and said, "Careful, do not touch,
this is art."
Look, her eyes are open wounds
without color or lashes
her mouth laughs and cries at once,
but why are her limbs scattered on the floor—
perhaps she is a joke?
And they asked, "Why is a rose
blooming from her neck?"
And someone murmured (it must have been you)
for something pretty and fragrant and true.
I felt each word
hitting my face like spit,
my head and torso
strung from a beam,
my limbs scattered on the floor
among the shifting feet of connoisseurs
nodding their heads, lordly savants,
and with eyes spraying ice,
they haggled my price.

SOMETHING ELSE

There is a place that we can reach
When our boats the sky will touch.
Even if we are silent or shout with pain
Kneel in obeisance or spit with rancor
    A deserted tree will not rustle welcome to us,
    A time-honed stone will not be our head rest
    The sea conceals hate-traps for us,
    The desert is a fire in our orphaned hearts.
    Of course, the error is entirely ours
    That's why even the night plays tricks on us.
    An anemic day rises fearfully toward us
    Nesting sparrows fail to recognize us
    Butterflies waft in malignant air, decidedly ignoring us.
    Children's eyes lacerate the ramparts of our hearts.
    We cast our eyes to the soil for hope
    The earth hides its face from us.
    Few might reach the seventh heaven
    Or the sixths or even the first
    And even fewer will behold
    The day when a new life will revive the dry bones.
    Only then will we recall the prophet's epitaph,
    Beat our breast and wail
    Why hadn't we hearkened to
    The words they said!

2

Even if we strain
We'll never reach an end
Again we'll stumble on another beginning.
Life is short, they say,
If so, why does each day stretch so long?
So exhausting, so void of hope,
So burning, so frozen?
It too shall pass, says the saint while he
Paces the room with furrowed forehead
And clashing brows, and with eyes
Empty of God he rubs his temples
With his saintly fingers
Proclaiming the end of the world.

3

Man looks at himself and is shocked:
Is this the marvel that with love
was created by God?
No, not with his hand, with a word:
Let there be! he proclaimed, and there was.
Is this his image we behold?
His reflection we uphold?
It is written that in his image he created us
Is that the reason man adores himself
In such an obnoxious way?

4

He comes toward me
Dripping rubies of sunset
His eyes reflect the great despair
His steps are halting, he limps, the slaughtered-God
Even his crown of thorns has lost its charm.
He walks the edge of the universe, on his
Lips a scream:
I am nailed to the cross of your heart
Years of many tears!
But man is deaf to the supplication of the—Great
For if man pulled out the nails
To who shall man pray?

5

When you say you love me
what exactly do you mean?
do you mean you love your
reflection in me?
you do not know me,
touch me and I'll disappear
and if my reflection
remains in your eyes
do not make the error
of believing that I am you
or inside you
you belong only

to yourself,
your wishes are
not mine
your actions do not
depend on me,
Love and lust,
two that are one,
you love me but your
hand caresses
your own
heart—
ahhh.

FORGET

Kisses of pale, barren spring.
One more leaf sinks into the sea of nights.
You're too tiny to live. Cease.
(It's impossible to contain the grief.)
Remove the membrane of birth and wipe
the blood off your face, you weren't born this moment.
Do you still carry my reflection in your heart?
A constant violence of love.
Radioactive rain impregnates heavy earth.
Sparrows nest in empty places.
Butterflies move on wings of steel.
A crevice of smile in a teary eye.
Yearning to love,
Yearning to be loved.
Always, always
Forget.

BURY ME, GABRIELA

When Gabriela came home that evening, she dropped her bag on the couch and walked to the window. Gazing at the oak tree, all she could think about was that day, a year ago, when she left her father at the hospital in Jerusalem to fly back to Boston to be with her husband, Neil. She remembered how immediately upon arriving home she had called her father's doctor.

"How is he?" she asked.

"Call your mother, Gabriela," he told her.

"He's dead."

"Yes, Gabriela, I'm sorry. He died a few hours after you left."

For a long moment, she just stood there, clutching the receiver in her hand until her fingers became numb. Vaguely, she heard the doctor's voice say, "Gabriela, are you there? Gabriela?"

All she could think of was that she had to go back to Jerusalem. She didn't unpack or even change her clothes. She didn't call Neil. She called the airlines and took the first flight back to her country. For fourteen hours she sat on the plane, and the only feeling she could remember was a sense of urgency burning inside her.

When she arrived at her parents' home, it was Friday. Her father's body was at the hospital's morgue. Stunned, she stood at the door. Her father wasn't buried yet and already her parents' home was crowded with people. What are they doing here? A rage filled her brain. She saw her mother, moving among the callers, bewildered and exhausted, her skin hanging like a rag on her face, gray rings etched under her eyes, and her hand clutching her chest from time to time as if trying to hush her heart. For a moment, Gabriela felt like a sharp stone had been turned round in her chest, but she wasn't able to attend to her mother. The tremendous feeling of urgency she felt throughout the flight turned into a feeling of suffocation;—she must see him now, immediately, to affirm with her own eyes that he was dead, to touch him, to ask his forgiveness for not being there with him in his last moments. The urgency was so great within her she could not lean upon the comforting illusion that she is dreaming and soon she'd wake up. Her friends were shocked when she said she wanted to go to the hospital now. "She lost her mind, they'll refuse to let her in," they whispered. "You can't go now," they cautioned her. Only her cousin, Daniel, a heart surgeon at Hadassa Hospital, took her hand. "I'll take you to see him," he said.

At the hospital, she walked along a gray concrete corridor, trembling with pity and anger, refusing to believe the fact that her father had passed through this corridor without her. She hadn't been there as she had promised, and she could make no amends now. She was overwhelmed by a sense of guilt and confusion.

When they reached the morgue, Daniel explained to the attendant that they came to see the body of Michael Wolk. She remembered well the attendant, a small man with a beak-like nose and shoulder-length side curls. A long black coat was hanging on him like on a hanger, and his body exuded odors of mildew and tobacco. "It's forbidden for the woman to be here," he muttered as he plucked at his long black beard.

"She's my responsibility," Daniel said.

The attendant pointed to a wall. "He's there," he said sourly. "But don't stay long, the Sabbath is coming. I'm closing at four."

"Please open it." Daniel said. The man pulled at a handle protruding from the wall, and the box glided out soundlessly. Her father's head appeared first. Like in birth, she thought. His body was covered with a white sheet. She uncovered his body, baring his chest. "Here he is," she heard herself say. She bent and kissed his forehead, his cheeks, delicately she passed her hand on his face, on his shut-eyes, on his slightly opened lips. His skin felt cold to the touch of her hands and lips, unnatural, but the feeling was not repulsive to her or even unpleasant. He was her father.

Daniel bent over and carefully opened the dead man's eyes. She gazed into her father's eyes. For a moment, she expected him to say, "Enough, Gabriela, let's go home." She waited, her hands two blocks of ice. After a while, she rested her cheek on his chest; but when her cheek touched his flesh, she burst out crying. Her entire body shook; chills ran down her spine. She told him she loved him, that she longed for their talks on lazy Sabbath days when he would sit in the soft leather chair and she on the floor, her back leaning on his legs, and his hand would caress her head. She told him how terribly she missed the times they used to spend riding through the flowering hills in winter, breathing the fragrance of wet grass. How she yearns for their walks between the narrow walls of the Arab market in old Jerusalem, inhaling the odors of musky perfumes and ancient spices. She told him how devastated she is not to have been with him when he died.

She talked for a long time. She heard Daniel call her name and felt his hand stroking her hair, and although she could not see him, she knew that he too was crying. Finally, she lifted her head off her father's chest and stood up. She remembered that as the saddest moment of it all, for she knew that now they would close the box, and she would never touch her father again. Full of sorrow, she looked at him. But she was not ready to grieve. Not yet.

Suddenly she saw two tears rolling down his face, leaving a silvery line on each cheek.

"Daniel, look," she said, "my father is crying."

She saw Daniel wince. "Let's go," he said and took her hand. But when she lingered, he said, his voice choking, "Gabriela, he isn't crying, he's thawing."

She stared at him with unblinking eyes. "If Jesus could rise from the dead," she said, "my father can cry in death." Daniel only smiled and squeezed her hand.

At that moment, the attendant came in. He seemed to swoop down upon them, his black coat flying wildly behind him. Dark and mean, he reminded her of a raven. He whispered something in Daniel's ear. Daniel took her hand and said they had to leave now.

With her frozen fingers, she wiped her father's tears then covered his body with the sheet.

On the day of the funeral, she was quiet and distant. But at night, stunned and lonely, she went back to the cemetery, gathered all the flowers from his grave, and brought them to the house. There she put them, without water, on the floor of his library.

During the next seven days, Gabriela looked after her mother. She ran like a maniac between the ringing phone and the screaming doorbell. An endless stream of relatives and people she didn't know came to pay their respect. Many wanted to know how life in America was and whether she was thinking of returning to Jerusalem. It was too bad, they had said, that Neil, her "wonderful" husband, couldn't come to the funeral; but Gabriela didn't explain. Those most concerned took her aside and wondered how her mother would manage. Maybe it will be better if she were to stay for a few months and take care of her—surely her husband will understand. Gabriela smiled and nodded. "Mother will be all right, thank you. It's so sweet of you to be concerned. You're so kind."

The days were chaotic. But at night, after everyone left and her mother took a sleeping tablet, she would go to her father's library; and there—among his pipes, books, and papers—she lived for a few hours among the aromas of her childhood. Nostalgia, like a drug, flowed through her veins. She sat in the dark, her hands caressing the polished wood of his desk. The windows were open, the night bright, and the scent of the jasmine wafted in with the whine of the jackals. Moonlight poured into the room, casting a blue shadow on the alabaster horse on her father's desk, the winged alabaster horse that seemed ready to leap toward the sky. Absently, she caressed it, caressed and waited.

It took the memorial flowers seven days to wilt.

A year had passed since then; and now on the anniversary of his death—in her home in Boston, so far from Jerusalem—she leaned her forehead on the windowsill and wept. "Yes," she said to the motionless tree as much as to herself, "I really believed that he was crying."

At night, she fell on her bed, determined but unable to subdue the pain. She tossed and turned; everything churned within her, shifting like desert sand in a windstorm.

Toward dawn, she fell into a deep, rapt sleep and dreamed *she was a little girl riding on a blue horse, her arms around her father's waist, her cheek pressing against his back. They ride through a field crimson with poppies. Butterflies—purple, yellow, and gold—fly around the horse's legs. A cool breeze plays with her hair, caressing her face. He and she are galloping toward the sun, and she is happy and light in the glittering air. But suddenly the red field becomes a sea of moving shadows. Black clouds sweep the vast expanse of blue sky. She clutches his waist tight, but he pries her arms loose and dismounts. She tries to follow him but is unable.*

*Don't leave me! she cries. How will I find the way in the darkness?
I miss you terribly, Father. Please stay. Gabriela, she hears his voice,
don't you remember? I am dead." A tide of darkness sweeps him
away. But, Father, she shouts, you can't be dead I didn't bury you.
She is shouting, but her voice is thin, scarcely a thread of a sound.
Silence. The only sound she hears is the drumming of her heart.
The blue horse gallops through the storm, and she holds tight to its
mane. Suddenly the horse stops. Neil, her husband, appears before
her. His hands are clasped in prayer, his face gleaming white and
wet. I knew you'd come back to me," he whispers. I'm so glad. And
she says, "No, you're no longer part of my life, I can't stay. A thick
mist envelops his face. Gabriela, my wife, we can try again. No!
Move out of the way! You're selfish, Gabriela. He continues to weep.
You were always selfish. He grabs her hand and tries to pull her
off the horse's back, but the blue horse gallops away, and Neil is
left cradling her severed hand to his heart. She wants to get off the
horse. She wants to retrieve her hand, but the blue horse is flying,
floating again in the dark through the storm. She must leave Neil
with something. She can do without her hand. And again the horse
halts, scraping its hooves along the ground. Sparks are flying in the
darkness. A full moon hangs suspended in space, illuminating the
blackness. The face of her lover Paul floats up toward her, radiant
in the darkness. Gabriela, he says, I knew you'd come you always
came back to me. No, she says, you left me, you went back to her
you lied to me. He laughs, come to me, my love. We'll be together
again, only you and me. His hand is on her chest, squeezing her
heart, and an awful sense of suffocation grips her. He tries to pull
her off the horse's back. But the blue horse bolts forward, and Paul,
her lover, floats in the air with her heart in his hand. I can't help
you, she whispers. I must bury my father. Give me my heart I can't
live without a heart. Gabriela! Gabriela!" The howling of the wind
and the shrill ringing of bells drown his rumbling voice. Gabriela,
you're so selfish, you promised to love me forever. The horse is flying
faster, the wind roars, the bells ring. Father! Father! She shouts*

and hears his voice. Faster. Don't listen to them, Gabriela. They'd all try to stop you. Go! Go fast! She holds tight to the blue horse's back, and both of them are swirling through endless space.

She woke up, terror in her heart, her body drenched, her eyes burning. The telephone by her bed was ringing.

"Hello," she said thickly, trying to shake off the dream.

"Gabriela, are you all right?" She heard Alexandra's voice, which brought her back to reality.

"I'm all right, Ali."

"Are you sure? Your voice sounds—"

"I don't want to talk now."

"What's happening to you, Gabriela?"

Silence.

"Gabriela?"

"I dreamed again about my father."

"You want to tell me?"

"I'll call you later."

"Would you like to meet for lunch?"

"It's so awfully hot outside."

"Gabriela?"

"All right." Gabriela paused. "Where would you like to meet?"

"The Garden? One o'clock. Would you like me to pick you up?"

"I'll take a cab." Gabriela hung up.

When Gabriela arrived at one fifteen, she found Alexandra sitting at a little table under a window, smoking a cigarette, and drinking gin and tonic. She flopped on the seat opposite Alexandra. "Sorry I'm late," she gasped, wiping her forehead. Alexandra smiled her slow, calming smile. She was a striking woman in her early thirties, a chief editor for a women's magazine. She carried a notebook in her bag and pads of tiny papers even in her little evening purse. Gabriela used to tease her about it, but Alexandra would merely smile slowly and say, in her mellow voice that sounded to Gabriela like an alto flute, "You may laugh, but one day you'll tell everyone that you know me." And Gabriela, with a mischievous glint in her eyes, would bow her head graciously and say, "I am honored to know you now, Ali." And they would laugh.

But they weren't laughing now. Sitting across the table from her friend, Alexandra observed the shadows in Gabriela's face. Her eyes were sunken, her hands trembling; even her black hair had lost its luster and hung limply around her face. "Brooding again, Gabriela?" Alexandra said. "Unable to sleep? To eat? You must learn to bury the dead. You can't carry a graveyard in your heart forever."

As she listened to her friend's voice and watched the light from the window flicker in her dark red hair, Gabriela felt something hard inside her soften. She smiled, but her eyes remained sad. "I could never bury my dead," she said. "Yesterday was one year since he died, and I couldn't even light a candle for his memory."

"Why not?"

"He hated rituals. He made me promise not to make a fuss over his death. He didn't want prayers to be said at his funeral, and he didn't want flowers on his grave. 'Beautiful things,' he used to say, 'belong to the living, not to the dead.' Of course, I couldn't prevent people from bringing flowers. My mother thought I was mad. I guess I was, a little. Perhaps I still am."

"And did you keep your promise?"

"Well, there weren't prayers at his graveside."

"What about the flowers?"

"After the funeral, I went and removed them from his grave."

"You removed the flowers from his grave?"

"Yes."

"I understand," Alexandra said. She lit a cigarette and smoked for a time in silence, then said, "Rituals are for the

101

living, not for the dead. Everyone, except you, seems to know that. He's dead. It's over. Don't you think that it's time to put the flowers back on his grave, light the memorial candle, and maybe even say a prayer or two? This is the way we mourn our dead."

"But I promised."

"He shouldn't have asked you to give such a promise. It was selfish of him." Alexandra gulped what was left of her gin and tonic.

"Perhaps," Gabriela said. "Yes, perhaps." But her anxiety didn't diminish; the dream haunted her. She kept hearing her father's voice saying, "Light doesn't enter eyes that are shut." But he was dead, and she could not go on pretending that he was alive. She must bury him.

"Are you going back to Jerusalem to visit your mother?" Alexandra asked.

"No. I don't think so."

"Any plans for the summer?"

"I don't know," Gabriela said, staring at the plate the waiter placed in front of her, fighting an upsurge of nausea. She placed the palm of her left hand like an open fan on her belly. She stared at her hand for a moment, thinking, this was the hand she left with Neil in the dream.

"I can't go, Ali," she said. "I just can't go." She felt as though a gigantic bird was pecking at her, tearing her flesh bit by bit, getting bigger and bigger, while she was shrinking, disappearing. "Am I ever going to get over all this?"

Alexandra struck a light. "Yes," she said after a moment, "I believe that you'll find what you're looking for, but it takes time. You must be patient." She blew out the match and didn't light her cigarette. She ordered another gin and tonic. "Gabriela," she said suddenly, "let's take a trip together. I need a vacation and so do you." Alexandra's face flushed; her voice rose a little. "It's a good idea," she said.

"A trip? Together? Where to?"

"To New York. You and I."

"New York? Why?"

"Why not?" Alexandra's eyes sparkled in anticipation. "It has been a long time since I have been in New York. I love that city, and I have a good friend there that I would like to visit. Come on." She grabbed Gabriela's hand. "It'll be fun. What do you say?"

"I don't know," Gabriela said, unable to overcome her melancholy. "New York is a mad place."

"Yes," Alexandra said, "many think so. But remember, it's not your mad place. We'll go fancy, celebrate. Say you'll come."

"But what if Paul calls?" Gabriela said in a small voice, embarrassed by her own words.

"Gabriela, for heaven's sake!"

"Okay, okay, I'll bury my dead," Gabriela muttered. She paused uncertainly. "When would you like to go?"

"What's wrong with today?"

"Today?"

"Why not?" Alexandra lit another cigarette. "Would you rather stay home and wait for Paul to call?" She leaned over the table. "Gabriela, Paul is back with his wife, and you have to face it. Go home and pack. I'll make the arrangements."

In spite of her doubts, Gabriela felt anticipation building up in her as the spirit of the adventure began to capture her fancy. "All right," she nodded, but all she felt were doubt and anxiety.

"We'll have a great time, Gabriela, you'll see." Alexandra signaled for the waiter and paid the bill. They walked into the street.

"Don't forget now," Alexandra said as Gabriela climbed into a cab. "I'll pick you up in two hours."

Gabriela shook her head. "Get rid of the graveyard in your soul," she admonished herself.

Within two hours, Gabriela was packed and ready. She went to the window and spoke to the oak, "Good-bye, old friend. I am going to have an adventure. Wish me luck." For a moment, she fancied that the wind picked up, and she saw the branches nodding in approval. "Crazy," she muttered. She heard the doorbell and ran downstairs.

At eight o'clock that night, they landed in New York.

Their taxi stopped at the Hotel Manifique. They were ushered to their suite. It was plush, luxurious, and grand.

"Magnificent," Alexandra exclaimed. She sat on a rose-colored velvet couch, rested her head against the pillows, and smiled contentedly.

Gabriela flopped into a wine-colored stuffed chair and curled her feet underneath her. She remained quiet.

"Don't you like it?" asked Alexandra.

"I don't know. It's so overly done—it looks fake."

Alexandra, laughing, lit a cigarette. "It's gaudy, pretentious, almost immoral, but it's great. So enjoy it."

They ordered drinks, not sure what to do next. They sat there as in a dream, sipping their drinks and watching the evening shadows play checkers on the plush furniture. Alexandra was savoring a double brandy. Gabriela, sipping white wine, was thinking, we're like two children playing at make-believe—Gabriela and Alexandra in fake land.

They had dinner at the hotel restaurant then returned to their suite. Neither of them wanted to go out.

Alexandra stretched out on the soft cushions of a rose velvet couch, sighed contentedly, and lit a cigarette.

"Tired of playing queen?" Gabriela said. She was sitting on the thick rose red carpet, leaning her back against the wall.

"Is that what I'm doing? Playing queen?" Alexandra said good-humoredly.

"Well," said Gabriela, "look around you. Dark red velvet chairs, rose velvet sofas, silk and velvet white curtains, rose red carpets, bronze sculptures, silk flowers—and marble. Marble everywhere—shiny rosy marble, smoky gray marble. Unreal! Did you see the bathroom? Black marble." Gabriela laughed nervously. "My mother should see me now. She would have hated this room. I can hear her say, 'Really, Gabriela, do you think you were born a princess? You're wild, child. Everything you do is wild. What am I going to do with you?'"

"Would she have really said that?" Alexandra asked, squinting her eyes at Gabriela.

"Well, something of this sort. My mother loved telling me that when I was brought to her in the hospital, she thought that they switched babies on her and gave her the wrong girl. She used to say that I'm not like the other children, that I was different right from the beginning." She sat meditating for a while. "You know, Ali," she said, "after the funeral, I couldn't connect with my mother. We remained distant. She still has not forgiven me for what I did with the flowers." After a moment, Gabriela smiled and said, "But my father used to say that I was the most beautiful, the most wonderful girl in Jerusalem, his one and only in the entire world." Gabriela stood up. She began pacing the room.

Alexandra sat up. "Would you have liked to live in Jerusalem? Maybe you should, at least for a while."

Gabriela stopped pacing and looked at her friend. "I don't know, Ali, I'm not sure. There was a time when I wanted to go back so badly that I hurt all over from being homesick. But then I married Neil, and he didn't want to live in Israel. And Paul, you know all about Paul. Then Father died. I don't know anymore, Ali. I just don't know." Her eyes narrowed as though they were looking across the sea all the way to Jerusalem.

Alexandra rose from the couch and hugged her friend's shoulders. "It's all right, Gabriela. Come on now, let's go to sleep," she said and steered her agitated friend toward the bedroom. Gabriela listened to the calming voice and relaxed a little. Finally, she fell asleep, but until she heard Alexandra's voice the next morning, she kept swaying between dream and reality.

"Good morning," Alexandra said brightly. "Here, have a cup of coffee. I have a phone call to make."

Gabriela sat up abruptly, almost spilling her coffee.

"Don't get so upset. It's only my friend Dorian," Alexandra said.

"The artist?"

"Yes, the artist." When she saw anxiety leaping into Gabriela's eyes, she said, "You'll like Dorian. He's a terrific person."

"I'm sure he is," Gabriela muttered. She sat up in her bed and drank her coffee slowly. She heard Alexandra talking on the phone.

"I miss you too, Dorian."

Gabriela heard Alexandra's special laugh.

"No," Alexandra said, "I'm not alone. My friend, Gabriela, is with me." Then she continued, "Yes, that'll be great. See you there." She laughed again, and with her hand over the mouth of the telephone, she turned to Gabriela and said, "We'll meet Dorian at nine o'clock tonight."

Gabriela slid back into her bed and covered her head with the blanket.

"I'm going to dress now," Alexandra said. "Are you coming?" She waited, but when Gabriela didn't answer, she left the bedroom and went back to the sitting room. She thought of calling Dorian and meeting him for lunch.

She didn't call Dorian. Instead, she spent the day writing in her journal:

Five o'clock. I am with Gabriela at the Magnificent in New. She is behaving strangely. She has become increasingly withdrawn and preoccupied. She is so quiet I worry about her. When I went in to see how she was doing, she jumped up. "I'm sorry to be such a bore," she said. "Why don't you go out, Ali?" I said it wouldn't be fun without her. She didn't answer. I closed the door behind me, but my heart felt heavy. I yearned to go out, but I couldn't bring myself to leave her. An hour later, she came in where I am writing and paced for hours. She is obsessed with the past. She talks about her father's death, her divorce from Neil, and about Paul. She still loves Paul. The bastard. But as Gabriela pointed out, "It takes two to make it or break it. Why blame Paul." Still I hate him. I don't think she would have left Neil if it were not for Paul. I wonder if she'll ever be able to let go of the past. Her whole world seems to have collapsed, when her father died. A whole year has passed since he died, but she blames herself for not being there with him. "Ali," she said to me, "if only I had been there! If I could have held him in my arms as he breathed his last breath, he would have exited this world with love! But I was not there, and he died without me. How horrible it must have been. Oh, Ali!" What a burden this must be for her. It gives me the creeps to hear her talk like this. She says that she doesn't believe in the continuation of the soul or in the afterlife. "When I die, Ali," she says, "I want to be buried under a tree, and I want lots of flowers, and I want everyone to make a big fuss over me,—have a great party." She has a thing about an old oak tree outside her window. She calls it "My Tree of Life." She says that she talks to the tree and that it talks to her. I wonder about Gabriela. I see fear in her eye, the confusion around her mouth, and the tremor of her hands. She talks about the center, the lost connection, and the severed umbilicus. "Ali," she cries, "I have lost myself!" Last night, I awoke suddenly and saw Gabriela tossing in her bed, talking in her sleep. I feel uneasy, as if something bad is going to happen. Maybe I should go alone to meet Dorian. Gabriela, like they say, is walking a tightrope, a sharp edge. I feel her pain acutely, but I don't always understand her. She is different; she is from a different place, a different world. Jerusalem. How exotic, so far away in place and time. I must go there one day. This trip has become unreal. It upsets me. I wish I knew how to help Gabriela.

Alexandra glanced at her watch. It was seven thirty, and at nine, they were going to meet Dorian. She went to the bedroom and found Gabriela sitting in bed, hugging her chest, her eyes closed. She was rocking in a rhythm that seemed ancient, elemental, and mindless.

"Gabriela," Alexandra said softly, afraid to startle her friend. Gabriela's eyes remained closed, but she stopped rocking. "Gabriela, open your eyes," Alexandra said and shook her friend's shoulders. Gabriela opened her eyes. She smiled slowly. her eyes, unfocused, seemed to look through Alexandra. Her face was tense and weary. Alexandra wanted to take her in her arms and hold her close but reined her impulse. She said, "Come on, snap out of it. It's time to get dressed. We should be leaving soon. Get up."

"Leaving?" whispered Gabriela.

"Don't you remember? We're going to meet Dorian at nine." Alexandra felt that she was losing her patience. She grabbed Gabriela by the hands and, not too gently, pulled her off the bed. To her surprise, Gabriela jumped off the bed; and in a few moments, Alexandra heard the shower turned on, and Gabriela singing in Hebrew at the top of her voice. Alexandra shook her head and went to get dressed.

Alexandra was ready and waiting. She was sipping a glass of wine when Gabriela emerged from the bathroom. Gabriela's face was clean of makeup. Her black hair, still wet, was tied behind her head, leaving her face and forehead naked. Tight blue jeans hugged her thighs while a white silk shirt tucked into her jeans emphasized her tiny waist.

"I should wear something more casual," Alexandra said. Suddenly she felt overly dressed, exaggeratedly made-up.

"Oh no, Ali, you look beautiful." Gabriela took Alexandra's hand. "Come on, let's go."

They decided to walk, but the night was damp and close and sticky. Outside, an oppressive heat enveloped them. They walked slowly, close together, along the unfamiliar avenues, between the roaring cars. They were surrounded by a multitude of people, blinded by gigantic neon lights. They repeatedly lost their way and couldn't find a taxi. It seemed, to them, forever until at last they reached their destination—a small bar on a small side street.

Looking around the room, squinting from the cigarettes' smoke, Gabriela's eyes rested on a man with unkempt, messy gray hair. He was sitting alone at a small table, absently drawing on a napkin. Preoccupied, he was oblivious to their approach. His large heavily furrowed face appealed to Gabriela; she felt drawn to him.

"Hello, Dorian," Alexandra said gently.

He looked up, and a smile lit his face. He rose and opened his arms. "Alexandra," he breathed her name. His voice was deep, and full of affection; and as he embraced Alexandra, Gabriela noticed how his face became full of light and charm.

Alexandra giggled; her cheeks glowed. For a minute, she stood wrapped in his arms. Finally, she disengaged herself and said, "Dorian, this is my friend, Gabriela." Dorian extended both arms to Gabriela. He held her hands, and they gazed at one another as though they were searching for hidden signals. Then he let go of her hands and smiled. "You're lovely," he said simply, stating a fact rather than paying a compliment.

"Thank you," she said, feeling a little self-conscious but not displeased.

He looked at Alexandra, and again the special smile transformed his face. "How wonderful to see you, Alexandra," he said. "Always elegant, always fresh, and cool. You bring peace, you make the world calm. You're a painting, you're a flower." He clasped her to him again and kissed her dramatically.

Alexandra blushed. "Oh, Dorian, you're embarrassing me," she giggled like a little girl.

While listening to Dorian's words, Gabriela recalled an old forgotten Hebrew song: *"Speak to me with flowers, my love, speak to me with flowers . . ."* She chuckled to herself. They sat down and ordered drinks. Gabriela gulped down hers, and the whiskey hit her in little explosions of warmth. She relaxed, and for the moment, the world seemed the way it should be. She ordered another drink, but this time she sipped it slowly. Dorian and Alexandra began to talk about their mutual friends then about her writing, but mostly he talked about his life as an unknown artist in New York. He talked as though he was painting, using different colors simultaneously, constantly changing shades, light, and hues.

"You understand," he said, "I strayed, I had to find a different way. I gave up my life as a successful artist in Boston because only money motivated me. I was possessed by pleasing rich people, producing 'art' to their liking." For a moment, he stopped talking and looked fixedly at Alexandra, his face looked stricken. They ordered more drinks. Gabriela felt a little drunk, and the world continued to seem okay. Dorian gulped his drink, leaned over the table, and in a hushed voice,—as though he were telling a secret,—said, "I felt as if my life were ending, as if I were dying. And so, I came to New York and began a new life. I am not successful, but I found myself. You understand, Alexandra?" He fixed his eyes on her, demanding her approval. "I had to come to this city and discover its beauty and its ugliness, its fascination and repulsion. Only here am I able to mix my colors not only with my hands but with my entire soul." For a moment, he stared at his hands, which were spread before him on the table as though they were two intruders. "In this place," he continued, "where I live unknown, I know myself, I feel me. I love, I laugh, I cry." He banged his hands on the table and shouted, "I am alive!" Then he fell silent, but his eyes continued to shine with a restless passion.

Listening to his wild talk, looking into his eyes, Gabriela felt the uncertainty in him, his self-doubt, and the effort he made to convince them and himself of the profound meaning and importance of his new life. She knew it was extremely important to him that they believed him, accepts him. He was like a desperate man pleading for his life.

"You understand me, Alexandra?" He turned to her again with the same urgent, insistent look in his eyes.

"Yes, Dorian, you're an extremely courageous man." She reached over and pressed his hand. "You've done well," she said.

Through her liquor-induced euphoria, Gabriela listened to Alexandra's voice. It seemed to her that Alexandra is playing a word game, yet she also understood the reason behind the game. Alexandra recognized the hand stretched out to her, and she held it.

"What do you think?" Dorian turned to Gabriela. She felt his hand on her knee, but she didn't move. His hand, through the thick material of her jeans, felt comforting. She didn't wish to talk. She wanted to stay quiet and savor the few moment of euphoria. "Talk," he insisted. She sat aloof, almost hostile, refusing to give in to him. Slowly she drank the rest of her whiskey, and when she finally talked, there was a challenge in her voice.

"What difference does it make what I think of your life, Dorian? You are talking as if you are in court. I'm neither your judge nor your jury. I don't pronounce verdicts of guilt or innocence. If you feel that this move was vital to your life, that New York makes the difference you long for; it is only you who knows the truth. Why ask me? Only a minute ago, you said that you've found yourself." She reined herself; her throat was dry, her lips numb. In her mind, she heard voices accusing her, *you're selfish, Gabriela, so selfish!* She saw the embarrassment in Dorian's eyes. For a moment, he looked at her as if she had struck him. He removed his hand from her knee.

"So that's the way you are," he said, "sharp at the edges."

But she didn't relent or soften. "Nonsense," she retorted; but at the same moment, she felt the sadness that flowed from him mixing with her own. Her mind, like his, ridiculed her; but regardless of how absurd he could be, he remained charming and attractive. And she was drawn to listen to him, to make sense of his confusion. Yet, while she understood the conflict in him, she went on. "You seem to justify your failure of the present and condemn your previous success. It's clear that you have not yet reached a real understanding of your move from success to loneliness. What rights do I have to interfere? Are you asking me to intrude upon your privacy, to violate your self-imposed isolation? This matter is between you and yourself alone."

Dorian gazed at her; his eyes reflected her anguish. Very softly, he said, "I'm lonely, you're right, but I also find strength in the solitary existence I imposed upon myself." And the same truth that she perceived in him earlier hit her again.

"I'm sorry, Dorian," she said.

He rested his hand very lightly against her cheek. A shudder shot up her spine, a familiar sensation. For a brief moment, she leaned her face on his hand. His touch felt rough and warm.

"Gabriela," he said, "you sound so sad."

"I have to light a memorial candle," she said.

He looked at her searchingly, as if trying to penetrate her thought. Then he nodded his head, and a strange understanding filled his eyes. They looked at one another as if they just woke up together from a mutual dream. She became acutely aware of the strength, love, and vitality that flowed from this man. At that moment, he seemed so much like her father that she was startled by a desire to put her head on his knees and feel his hand caressing her head, but she only smiled, grateful for his understanding.

Through the dim light in the smoke-filled bar, Alexandra watched their faces clouded with sadness. She was struck with deep tenderness for them. She listened to their conversation, not missing a word. The moment belonged to Dorian and Gabriela. Understanding this, she sipped her wine, smoked her cigarette, and smiled at them with quiet affection.

Later they stopped in quiet and intimate little bars. They drank all night, and their heads pined. They walked the empty streets of New York in the early-morning hours, their eyes burning, their souls longing. "You're so soft," Dorian whispered in Alexandra's ear, his arm around her waist. He brushed his lips against Gabriela's neck. A delicious sensation filled her body; the old familiar shudder shot up her spine again. She disengaged herself from Dorian's claiming arm and walked ahead. Alone. But once alone, her euphoria changed to restlessness. Like a sleeping beast, the city lay in front of her, ready to pounce and sink its claws into her flesh. Her father's face floated before her, white like wax with a tear rolling down his dead cheek, and the dawn, like a ghost, rising over the sleeping city. She halted and waited until she felt Dorian's arm hugging her shoulder.

"Come to the hotel for a last drink," Alexandra invited Dorian.

"Wonderful," roared the artist.

Gabriela sensed immediately the tension in his body.

When they entered the suite, Dorian stood stunned; then after a moment, carried on by his excitement, he walked around the room as if moonstruck, delicately touching with the tip of his fingers the little statues as if he were touching a woman's body. His sensitive hands felt the thick velvet curtains; he stroked the pink marble, which seemed to radiate warmth under his touch. "Magnificent," he whispered, "What a fantasy. I wish to stay forever in this dream." The artist closed his eyes. And indeed, at that moment, a shimmering light, which gave it the illusion of a magical splendor, had suffused the room.

And while Dorian was immersed in his orgasmic excitement with the splendor of the room, Alexandra changed into a long black satin dress and reclined on the soft pillows of the velvet sofa. Gabriela changed her jeans into a blue silk caftan and joined them.

Dorian stared at them, his eyes glinting in anticipation.

Gabriela began to dance. She moved slowly, her bare feet moving to an inner rhythm, the silk of her long caftan making a swishing sound. Her face was white, her loose hair covering her shoulders, her green eyes half-closed. She seemed like an image from a different time, a different world.

"Dance for me," whispered Dorian. He circled her, slowly entering the dance, not touching her.

"Speak to me with flowers, my love, speak to me with flowers," Gabriela sang softly.

Suddenly Dorian emitted a short laugh and turned to Alexandra, and with his eyes fixed on hers, he swiftly took off his clothes. He stood there as naked as he can be. "Alexandra! Gabriela! Come to me!" He called out to them, intoxicated by a sense of his masculine power. Gabriela stopped dancing. For a moment, she stood rooted to the floor. A dull anger made her tremble slightly, but at the same time, a fire started to glow in her blood. She looked at Alexandra. Alexandra, who was reclining on the sofa's pillows, didn't move. Her bare face, neck, hands, and feet shimmered against the intense black of her dress. Gabriela's eyes turned to Dorian. It was clear to her that he was aware of the excitement that beat in their blood. He stood erect, faint waves rippling the muscle of his bare arms.

Gabriela was waiting. Alexandra was waiting. Dorian was waiting.

Then, like two thieves, Alexandra's hands crept to her throat; and she began to unbutton her dress. But in spite of herself, she was more aware of Gabriela's presence in the room than of Dorian. She looked pleadingly at her friend, but Gabriela's face was expressionless, her eyes fixed on Dorian. Alexandra hesitated for a moment. She shifted her eyes from Gabriela to Dorian. Then she dropped her hands to her sides, leaving the top of her breasts exposed.

The two women were paralyzed as if drugged. They felt cold while their bodies were throbbing, hot. They resisted with all their might his offering of love. Alexandra's perfect stillness turned to agitation. She willed her body to stay completely rigid for fear of trembling. Gabriela's face was a mask. Dorian's arms reached out to Alexandra. "Alexandra!" Her body leaned toward him, but her face was perplexed, forlorn. Again, she looked at Gabriela. "I'm sorry, Dorian," she muttered, her voice cracking.

She leaned back on the pillows of the sofa.

Dorian's face hardened. A momentary rage stormed through him, leaving his proud body shaking, shrinking. He didn't know what to do with his naked limbs and had the sorry appearance of a child caught in a forbidden game. He sat huddled in the deep velvet chair, wishing he could disappear. And thus, they stayed, completely silent.

But despite her embarrassment, his anguish stabbed at Gabriela. She wanted to reach out to him, comfort him, but she didn't move. The room became suddenly ridiculous in its jaded extravagance. Alexandra's face was empty of expression, her eyes wandered from Gabriela to Dorian, and her fingers mechanically buttoned up her dress.

Gabriela was cold, her throat shut. Alone in her pain, she returned to her dead.

Dorian's face was etched with dark furrows, his hair disheveled. He put on his clothes and left without a word.

Outside, a cool morning wrapped itself around him. The wakening city welcomed him. New York. His city. He threw back his head and spread his arms. "I'm alive!" he roared into the fading night. His spirit soared. He felt happy. He'd go to his studio and paint the two women just as he left them,—sitting there frozen like the ridiculous statues that decorated that sumptuous room. The thought filled him with renewed excitement, and he hastened his pace, eager to start his new work.

At the Hotel Manifique, an awkward silence fell upon Gabriela and Alexandra, their faces drained in the dim light of dawn. Gabriela was sitting on the floor, staring at space, and the voices screamed in her head:

Gabriela, we can try again.
You promised to love me forever, Gabriela.
Let's take off our clothes, Gabriela.
Bury me, I am dead, Gabriela.

Alexandra buried her face in her hands. "I don't understand what just happened," she whispered. For a long moment, Gabriela gazed at her, keeping her silent. With an impatient gesture, Alexandra wiped her tears. "Did he really expect us to make love with him?"

"Don't you really know?"

"He must have thought so," Alexandra said.

"You wanted him," stated Gabriela.

"And you didn't?"

Gabriela didn't answer. She rose from the floor, sat down on a chair, then stood up and again wandered about the room.

"Sit down already!" Alexandra almost screamed.

But Gabriela didn't listen. Alexandra's question pestered her: did Dorian arouse her? Did she want him? "Yes," she finally answered, "I wanted him." And when Alexandra didn't answer, she asked, "You feel as if you betrayed him?"

"Yes, that's exactly how I feel!"

"Then why didn't you make love with him?"

Alexandra flinched at the vehemence in Gabriela's voice. "I was afraid," she said hesitantly. "I was unable to move."

"Why?"

"I don't know," she said, rubbing her temples. "For years, I have wanted to make love to Dorian, and now, when all I had to do was reach and take, I couldn't move. I feel so ashamed. He seemed so lonely."

"So what? Didn't he say that he enjoyed his loneliness that loneliness is an inseparable part of the self-awareness and freedom he had found? Think about it, Ali."

"You're cruel, Gabriela," Alexandra flared up. "Try to be more forgiving. Whenever you fail to understand someone, you become cruel. Don't you feel compassion for Dorian? Don't you care?"

"You have got it wrong, Ali." Gabriela's smile was bitter. "Whenever I fail to understand myself, I become cruel. Like how it was with Neil."

"Neil? Don't change the subject, Gabriela. We are talking about Dorian."

"Really?" Gabriela said in a dull voice, focusing inward. She saw Dorian's naked body erect and proud one moment, shrinking and lifeless in the next. A kaleidoscope of images blitzed her mind. Here was Neil, her husband, crouching on his hands and knees like a dog, and she is lying on the floor beneath him, screaming, "I hate you! I hate you!" Then she is with her lover, Paul, their bodies slippery with sweat. Her pleasure is immense; her heart is pounding like a million drums. And here is Alexandra, reclining on the velvet sofa's pillows, reaching her arms to touch Dorian's nakedness; and she sees herself observing them with a fake mockery. And now she is sitting by her father's bed, and he says to her, "Don't pray on my grave, Gabriela. Don't bring flowers. Beautiful things are for the living, not for the dead." And she's tied to a winged blue horse, shouting, "Don't leave me, Father, I haven't buried you yet!"

"Gabriela, talk to me," she heard Alexandra's voice.

"Magical trick," Gabriela said.

"What?"

"It was a magical trick, but the magic failed."

"What do you mean?"

"It was all an illusion. It wasn't real. That's the reason we couldn't participate. Why feel sorry for Dorian? He acted his part perfectly," she continued without taking her eyes off Alexandra's face, which was staring at her, bewildered. "Why feel guilty?" she continued. "We were tricked into believing that he was offering his soul and body to the gods, and we are the high priestesses, his brides. The three of us sacrificing ourselves on the altar of love." Gabriela closed her eyes; and for a long moment, she stood there, swaying slightly. "Ali," she said, making a tremendous effort to control her voice. "Would you like to make love to me? Is that what you really want?"

"Yes," Alexandra said.

"And because of me, you couldn't join with Dorian?"

"No, Gabriela, it wasn't because of you. It was because of myself."

Gabriela lowered her eyes for a moment, then looked at her friend, and smiled apologetically. "I'm sorry, Ali, but . . .—"

"I know," Alexandra interrupted her. After a moment, she asked, "Is everything all right between us now?"

"Of course, everything is all right between us, Ali. Between us, it's always all right." They regarded one another, and a new kind of intimacy flowed between them, a new perception. They sat there in silence, each one struggling to resolve with herself the confusion she got into, to try and express her thought in words.

"I still feel miserable about Dorian, he looked so humiliated," Alexandra said. "Maybe I should call him and apologize."

Gabriela leaned back in her chair. "No, Ali, not now." After a moment, she said, "Do as you want."

"Gabriela . . .—," Alexandra began, but Gabriela interrupted her.

"Poor Dorian," she said. "He tried to convince himself and us that he was genuine, and for a while, he succeeded. It was only after he left that I knew it wasn't true, that he was unreal like this room." Suddenly her anger dissolved. She felt wasted, terribly weary. "Poor Dorian," she whispered. "Maybe I did him injustice, maybe I was wrong. And he was true to himself. I refused to understand and accept him because nakedness of this sort is threatening to me. It's too real, too painful. I missed the moment, Ali, and I missed a chance to love." Gabriela's face was tense, but a new strength began to glow in the depth of her eyes. "I should have made love with Dorian, Ali. I know I should have,—and you too. What's more natural than one's naked flesh? It's basic, primordial. We are born this way. He wasn't deceiving me he was real. I wasn't. I pretended that it wasn't important, that I wasn't interested."

"You should have seen the expression on your face, Gabriela," Alexandra said. "Mockery? Disdain? You who is in search of the center, the umbilicus, the lost connection." She leaned back on the sofa's pillows, lit a cigarette, and closed her eyes.

Gabriela leaned forward. "But isn't he searching for those exact same things?" she cried passionately.

She got up and wandered about the room. Her chest tightened in pain, and everything inside her seemed to stand still for a moment. Then, a sense of relief came upon her as if a shadow of a bird of prey has been lifted from her body, removing its claws from her chest, making her able to breathe. She turned to her friend.

"Ali," she called, "I'm going . . ."

But Alexandra,—spent by her tumultuous eruption of emotion, the burning cigarette almost scorching her fingers,—was fast asleep. Carefully Gabriela removed the cigarette and extinguished it in the ashtray.

She walked across the room to the window and watched as the morning fog dissipated to the light of the morning sun. Suddenly a single image caught her eye. Far below on the bridle path of Central Park, a man was riding on a horseback. And there, for one moment, as man and horse rode away into the haze of morning, she was sure that the horse was blue.

INTANGIBLE MEETING

At the very core of the night he came,
he uttered not a word, only
stood there, head bowed,
his body exuding malignant sorrow.
The next night he came again,
in the eye of night he came:
melancholic and silent he stood
before me in the dark
and I was afraid to ask why he came.
But when on the third night he appeared
I was waiting for him, awake,
my mind quivering and tense:
"Is it you? Say, is it you?"
But of course I knew who he was.
He lifted his eyes
a pale smile wept over his face
he looked at me with pained eyes,
he stretched to me shadow arms.
I arose from the bed
and floated to him on the dusky, dark air,
but he melted away.
(A faint scent of tobacco and rosemary lingered)
And I remained alone in the night
aching for the solace
of light.

WITHOUT A HAND

He lived without a hand,
His brain embedded in a dream,
He existed inside a fog of ideals.
He lived. I loved him without understanding.
He died. I didn't understand.
He didn't even say good-bye.
His life experience ceased.
My life is sadder without him.
His body is embedded in the earth
His body,
Without
A hand.

CHILD OF MANY YEARS

Time suicides in you, also in me.
Perplexity of years, fire of forgetfulness.
The grass is seared, but you are still
Clearing way to beauty,
Drunk with life.
This music is
Madness in you too,
Wandering the light,
Entering the night
Child of many years
So beautiful.

CRAZY SUN

I told you
It is a crazy sun
Lemon trees consumed
Burning paths on their way
I am pulled to the center of light in you,
In the vortex of consciousness
You are a glowing gallop
In the abyss of my youth
You are an orchid
Of the sun.

WORDS

Wandering in the vortex of consciousness
I thank you for a meager word.
In the archives of memory
You have many words.
Wandering inside my years
Sorrow seeps into earth
That from blight does not absorb moisture.
Meager words.
Disconnecting from its bondage,
My spirit wanders outside time
Gliding distances without moving
Dragged into the unknown.
Decayed love in the archives of memory.
Not a flicker from youth remains.
Anemic words. Meager words.
In the archives of life.

ONE SHOULD BE ABLE TO CRY

One should be able to cry.
You do it in secret.
Insulted and estranged
You walked heavily
Inside the fortress of silence
You imposed upon yourself.
The doves still chatter on the
Roof of your house in the mornings
And each day paints a fresh wrinkle
In the face of the loneliness with which you
Veiled your days.
Let the tears cool the
Burns of longing to those
That death had devoured.
Free your tears from metal,
Your roar will shatter heavens.
What am I without you?
Your voice brings beauty back to me
I still hear the two of us
Singing *"Brilliant Childhood"*
But even then, in the light
Loneliness stalked you—
Also me.

DESERT DANCE

(LIAT)

Since dawn, Pauline has been trying to capture Liat's face on canvas. Fatigued and disheartened, she pours herself a glass of red wine and lights a cigarette. She collapses into her soft black leather chair, looks through the window at the darkening sky, watching the evening veil the heavy city with its soft shadows, and tries to empty her head from pestering thoughts. Slowly she sips her wine and watches the shadows play checkers on the furniture. The wine makes her drowsy. She is sliding into sleep when suddenly the doorbell rings. Pauline doesn't stir; she isn't interested to see anyone now. The doorbell continues to ring. She continues to sit motionless for another moment then sighs and, a little heavily, gets up. "So much for relaxation," she says to the shadows as she goes downstairs to open the door.

"What took you so long?" Liat says and walks past Pauline into the living room.

Since Liat's marriage to Philip not quite a year earlier, Pauline doesn't see much of her. It isn't that she has a grudge against Philip; on the contrary, Philip is a brilliant man. So brilliant that he tends to make people around him feel inadequate, even a little stupid. At times, he is gentle and caressing in sort of a big-catway; and at times controlling, cynical, patronizing, and contradictory. When Pauline is in the same room with him, she is aware of his presence more than anyone else. The first time she met him, he said that she should be a fashion model instead of wasting time being a painter. "Everything worth painting has already been painted," he said in his deep sardonic voice, looking at her amusedly and gripping her hand much too long. Pauline was surprised when Liat married Philip. He's in his late forties, Liat, in her twenties. Liat doesn't talk about it, so Pauline doesn't ask. Still she thinks it was a strange choice, and immediately she admonishes herself: What do I really know about her? Who am I to judge others?

Now she hears Liat say, "It's so dark in here, Pauline. It makes me nervous." And immediately she turns on all the lights in the room. "Give me a cigarette," she says. "What's the matter with these matches? My eyes feel like pins have been stuck in them. This insomnia is driving me crazy."

"Relax," Pauline says and lights a fresh cigarette. She watches her friend pace the room. "Please, Liat," she says, "Sit down. Would you like a drink?"

"No thanks," says Liat.

"Something is wrong? Did something happen with Philip?" Pauline's voice is low and her eyes soft.

Liat flops down on the sofa. "Everything is wrong," she says. "These endless nights, hour after hour, lying on a bed of sand trying to speed up time, praying for daylight to come and erase the dread of the nightmares. In the dream, I hear machine guns jarring, and I want to scream that I am not to blame, but I only whisper that I didn't mean it to end like that. Everyone is dead, and the dead don't listen. Open dead eyes stare at me accusingly. And I hear this shrill supernatural laughter, and I see endless open space of white desert, and dust fills my throat and mouth, and I am sinking deep into the dust. My hands are clutching my ears, but I can't escape the laughter and the blurred images that are chasing me. Suddenly I am being squeezed between two enormous wings—Philip's arms. I struggle to get away, but I am not able to move. Philip's breath is spewing scorching fumes on my neck, but then in the dream, I know that it isn't Philip at all, and I wake up remembering, and my stomach fills with stones."

Liat is silent.

Pauline is anxious that her silence will be long. It is also clear to her that the dream stirred in Liat something deep, painful, and urgent, something she must get rid of.

"Did you tell Philip?" she asks.

"When I told Philip, he said that I am now in America, and there are no wars in America. Everything is all right in America; there is nothing to worry about. I thought, what a stupid thing to say, not at all worthy of Philip. And because he thinks that sex resolves most problems, he began to kiss and caress me, then laid his huge body on mine and moved above me, growling like a lion, his sweat dripping onto my face. I shut my eyes tight, and made a tremendous effort not to cry. When he was finished, he held me for a while and then fell asleep, and I lay there facing him, feeling confused, discouraged, listening to his breathing and watching his bearded, lion-like face, thinking, whom was I fooling? Not Philip. After a while, I got up and left the bed and went to the spare room where I have been spending my nights alone more often than not, writing letters that I never send."

"Why don't you send the letters?"

"What difference does it make?" Liat says impatiently.

Pauline nods her head and smiles in a placating way.

"When I stopped writing, I realized it was morning," Liat continues as if to herself. "I heard the birds beginning to chirp, and I relaxed a little. I even began to think that the dream is only a hallucination of my overwrought imagination and that nothing bad happened.

"Philip gets furious when I spend the night in my workroom. 'It's insulting,' he says. 'A wife should sleep with her husband.' And I try to explain and argue and plead that it isn't his fault, that I get restless because of the nightmare, and I am afraid to disturb his sleep. But he insists that I don't love him, and he's still angry. It doesn't make sense. Why can't he understand that I can't sleep? He keeps declaring how much he loves me. He says that I am his life. 'My gem,' he calls me. How is it possible that he loves me so much and doesn't even try to understand me?"

"We don't always understand the people we love most," dares Pauline.

"I know," says Liat, "and I don't pretend to understand Philip. I don't know why I love him. Perhaps he's right. Perhaps I don't love him. All I know is that he touches my soul."

"I know what you mean," says Pauline.

"Really? Then you know more than I do. I can't explain it. Maybe it means nothing, and maybe it means all, and Philip is also a part of the nightmare."

"What's happening to you, Liat?" asks Pauline.

"I am homesick. So, so homesick," says Liat, her voice choking. "Sometimes I wish I had stayed in the army like my brother and forget this rotten real world."

"How was it to serve in the army?" asks Pauline, trying to divert Liat's mind away from her trouble with Philip.

Liat runs her fingers through her short black hair. Her eyes are fixed somewhere above Pauline's head. "You always want to know about my time in the army," she says after a moment and gives Pauline a suspicious look.

"I am interested," says Pauline. "I don't know anything about women in the army."

"You don't miss a thing." Liat emits a short, humorless laugh.

"Nevertheless," says Pauline. She feels restless; she knows Liat isn't inclined to talk about her experience in the army. She lit a fresh cigarette.

"I almost got killed once," says Liat suddenly.

"Seriously?"

"Did I ever tell you what happened in the desert?"

"No," says Pauline.

"Of course not. I never told you. I've never told anyone. Not even Philip. I really wanted to tell Philip because when I married him, I thought we'd be able to talk about everything. How naive of me. But he'd seemed so wise and understanding, so big and comforting and deeply psychological. But soon he became jealous of everything that had to do with my past or with my country. Lately he's been watching me in this queer way,—somewhat cagey, a little evasive. And when I asked him why he looks at me like that, he said, 'what way? You're imagining things again.' And I begin to doubt myself. Perhaps he's right, perhaps I am imagining things."

"Maybe he is right?" says Pauline.

"Maybe. Maybe I am going mad. He tells me to go do something constructive instead of standing for hours staring out the window at nothing. Few days ago, he came and stood with me, hugged my shoulders, and asked, 'what is it, Liat? What do you see out there?' I said that I see the desert. 'Desert?' he asked. 'What desert? Come back to me.' I said that I'm here. 'No,' he said, 'you're not here, you're there.'

"When I didn't answer, he sighed and took his arm off my shoulders, then silently went to his study and banged the door behind him. Imagine, he blames me for being frigid. My god, if he only knew about the fire that consumes me."

Liat is silent.

Pauline gets up and turns off all the light in the room. She leaves only one lamp lit on the table next to the couch where Liat is sitting, then goes back and sits in her chair.

"What time is it?" Liat asks suddenly.

"Almost midnight," says Pauline. She scrutinizes Liat's face. She knows that something difficult is happening in her friend's life. Liat's eyes are sunken and also too bright, a little frantic. She is pale, and her hands tremble.

"Almost midnight," Liat whispers. "Time to dream again. To dream about the excitement I had then in that desert. This excitement is like a drug in my blood, a perpetual desire to play with death. I spend hours fantasizing, reenacting, reliving every moment of that day. It is as though my body has a memory of its own, and the year is still 1953, and the summer rules over sky and sea. And I'm eighteen years old, serving my term in the army, six months into a special training course for military instructors in a camp that used to be a British barrack, perched on a hill by the Mediterranean with the ruins of the gray cement buildings still scattered all over the beach like giant seashells." During the day, the place was dazzling with the white beach below the hill and the low waves lazily foaming and softly purring. And above the sea, the sky, so blue, stretching out to infinity. And in these magical surroundings, we trained all day and often at night, with the sea breeze always chasing after us. You see all seems possible when you're eighteen,—strong, full of ideals, and so enthusiastic. We trained hard, men and women together. We did almost everything together, but we slept in separate barracks, which wasn't a big problem because about ten minutes after lights-out, I would sneak onto the beach and meet my boyfriend among the ruins of the old British buildings and swim naked in the welcoming sea. Once I was caught and had to stay after training in the barracks for a week. It meant no entertainment and no freedom to move about the camp, that was a little rough. My boyfriend at that time was Danny Oren, one of the officers. A vain and fatuous man, but absolutely gorgeous as they say here in America. It was all so stimulating, so new, and the summer lasted forever and smelled of sea and sand and innocence, and we were all tanned and beautiful and looked as if we were drenched in honey.

My face was painted with freckles as big as copper coins, and there was a lot of gold in everyone's hair and in the air, so much gold that even the moon seemed golden instead of silver. And we never slacked off on our training. The competition was fierce. Everyone had to be the first, the bravest, the fastest, and the strongest. Every one of us wanted to be the best. I was the best sharpshooter—forgive me for bragging. I won a medal, and my name was mentioned in the newspapers as the only female competitor among hundreds of men. It was fantastic. My ego was inflated to the point of bursting. Everything seemed possible then, and I was going to live forever. And then suddenly, the summer and the training course were over—and the fun. Even the sky and the sea seemed duller. I was made a corporal and said good-bye to Danny Oren, solemnly promising never to forget him and yes, yes, of course I'd write. I'd write to everyone. The next day, I boarded a bus heading to the desert city of Beer-Sheba where I was to be stationed. My assignment was to train a group of young men before they reached the age of eighteen and went into the service. The idea was that they would be prepared when they joined the regular army and would save time in basic training. And so I was stationed in Beer-Sheba and assigned to work in a new village inhabited by Moroccan Jews and situated in the Arava desert, about five miles north of the city. I was briefed about the job by my new commanding officer, a small compact man in his early thirties, immaculately dressed, who even in the worst heat he carried himself erect as small people sometimes do in order to give an impression of being bigger than they actually are. Two days after I arrived in Beer-Sheba, he drove me to the village to meet the group of boys I was to train.

And in the jeep on the way to the village, I remember him watching me with a look I couldn't quite fathom at the time.

One minute his forehead would crease with worry, and he would shake his head. Then he would chuckle to himself and look as if he had remembered a joke he wouldn't share with anybody. As we approached the village, he looked less amused and more apprehensive, and I felt nervous too. The mystery was soon over. We arrived at the village, which consisted only of a few wooden huts and some anemic-looking desert shrubbery. On one porch, a few old men were playing backgammon and drinking ark from filthy glasses. It was noon time so apart from them the place seemed deserted. But as I jumped off the jeep, I saw a group of young men standing by a water tower, yelling, laughing, shoving one another, and looking like mental patients who had escaped from an asylum.

"Here they are," my commanding officer said. He approached the boys and told them to get in line, which they did reluctantly, grumbling. They were dirty and sloppy, their bodies exuding an overwhelming odor of sweat and garlic and something else that I couldn't identify just then;—later I became familiar with the taste and smell of hashish. And when my commanding officer introduced me as Corporal Liat Erez, their new instructor, a sudden silence fell over the entire group, as if a machine gun had suddenly stopped firing. They stood gaping at me, uncomprehending yet curious, with sort of a weird, black-browed amusement as apes in a zoo gape at visitors. And I stood facing them not sure what to say or how to handle the situation because this wasn't the army, and I couldn't have expected to be obeyed by giving orders. I knew I had to gain their trust and make them respect me, but I felt utterly confused. They were big and dark and rough-looking in kind of a cocky, shabby way. I looked at my commanding officer for help, but he only shrugged as if to say, "They're all yours."

So I said, "Shalom," and hoped for the best. I asked the first boy on the left, a small thin creature with crooked rust-colored teeth and tiny deep-set eyes that glittered like new thumbtacks, his name.

"Didi," he said, and they all burst into hilarious laughter, shoving and poking one another, while Didi danced around looking like a mad thing in the night.

Then a tall dark boy with oily black curls and wild eyes smiled at me crookedly. "What is it? A kindergarten? What do I see? A little girl. How old are you, sweetie? Ten? Twelve?" He said all this in a creamy voice, and through puckered lips, he blew little kisses in my direction. The boys doubled over, shrieking like lunatics. All I wanted was to stop their laughter and this unexpected mockery of my authority. I wanted to smash that smiling face into tiny pieces and grind the pieces into the dust with my foot, but I didn't move. I stood erect in front of them, determined to win the moment, and asked the dark boy his name. He only continued to smile. I strove to find words to save my honor, but all the clever words I had rehearsed vanished from my brain, evaporated into the boom of the desert heat. It felt as if I were watching a play yet being inside it at the same time. I remember thinking, Am I dreaming this?

Finally, unable to think of anything, I shouted, "Shut up! Just shut up!" To my surprise, the tall one with the oily curls stopped smiling and slowly straightened up. He fixed his eyes on me with a long, penetrating look. I held my head high and glared back. I saw that the boys stopped laughing and stood motionless. Only Didi broke every now and then into what sounded like a shriek, but he stopped immediately after a look from the tall boy with the oily curls.

"I am Emil," the boy said, and I saw him look at his hands. The fingernails were bitten and bloody, and the hands were filthy. As if embarrassed, he rubbed them on the sides of his torn jeans.

"Emil," I said.

"Yes," he said and again gave me his brilliant smile.

135

"I'm appointing you to be in charge of this group. Now get everyone in line. I want to talk to all of you."

And Didi mimicked me, "Yah, Emil. Yah yah. She wants to talk to you."

And I heard Emil say, "Shut up, Didi," but his voice was deep with affection. I didn't feel half as sure as I hoped I sounded. I felt dirty and crumpled. My hair was sticky and damp and stuck out from under my cap, pricking my neck. And I was dripping with perspiration. All I wanted was to go home and take a bath. These boys were far from anything I had ever known, so poor and primitive—almost illiterate, utterly undisciplined. To me, born and raised in Kibbutz Regev, they existed only in stories or in movies. Who was I to walk into their lives? I had to remind myself constantly that I was a soldier in the Israeli army, and these boys were my responsibility.

Once Emil got the group in line, they stood ill at ease, some kicking at little stones on the ground, others scratching their heads, and some only standing awkwardly with their hands in their pockets, looking at me blankly. No one laughed, not even Didi, and I wasn't sure I liked it. I heard the wind whine, and I shivered.

Then Emil said, "Commander Liat, we are ready." And as he stood at attention—saluting me, with his pelvis and belly thrust out, his shoulders hunched, his chest caved in;—he looked so comical. It was my turn to laugh. Yet at that moment, looking at him, I was aware of a floating sensation, a fascination. At the same time, I noticed that all of the buttons on his shirt, except one, were missing, so I didn't laugh. I stood staring at him for a long time, probably holding my breath, for I remember feeling dizzy. He just stood there and continued to smile at me brilliantly, perhaps a little mockingly. I wasn't sure, I wasn't sure of anything. The heat was so intense I felt as if I were melting.

I knew that Emil was making fun of me when he saluted me in such a theatrical way. Yet, from that time on, he called me Commander Liat. Later he said that it made him feel good to call me commander and that it gave me importance. "Don't be offended," he said, "if we call you commander, you look much bigger and more important—even if you are only a girl."

Soon the boys came to the training sessions dressed in clean clothes, their hands, and faces scrubbed. They quickly learned to drill and to use different weapons, but their favorite time was the night training, orientation by the stars. We had such a good time, many laughs and good feelings. Everything was going great. And after a while, I even got used to Didi and came to like him. Didi was Emil's shadow. Where Emil went, Didi went. What Emil said, Didi repeated. Didi had been orphaned when he was ten years old. He didn't have brothers or sisters. He didn't have anyone. And Emil had convinced his mother to let Didi come live with their family. "It didn't really matter," Emil had said, "because there are thirteen of us, and one more wouldn't make any difference." It didn't take much to convince his mother. And so, Didi moved in with Emil's family and became one of the clan.

Sometimes I would visit Emil's mother. I would sit in the shade of her neat little hut drinking spicy tea brewed especially for me, and we would chat. When I asked her about Didi, she said that after a while, she didn't even remember that Didi wasn't her own child. But sometimes,—when Didi would behave completely nuts, as she put it,—she would forget herself and say, "I don't believe I gave birth to such an ugly thing," and then she would remember and squeeze Didi into her gigantic bosom. And with tears in her eyes, she would say that she loved him as much as she loved her own children. But it wasn't Didi she was concerned about. It was Emil. "He's very wild," she would say. "Wild like a big black animal. He gets in much trouble. Much trouble. You talk to him. He thinks you okay."

She would say this in a kind of a stage whisper, and looking at me in a conspiratorial way, she would shake her head, click her tongue, and spit against the evil eye.

Emil was everyone's favorite. The people in the village idolized him, perhaps also feared him a little,—feared the toughness of his manners, his raw and, at times, violent temper. When people didn't know him, they could never decide how to take him, and yet they loved him.—And so did I.

But things weren't as smooth as all that, and all wasn't as wonderful as I—in my enthusiasm and naïveté—was determined to believe then. Boys from different villages around Beer-Sheba formed gangs and fought one another, and sometimes the fights were so fierce that boys were severely injured. Instructors were strictly forbidden to go alone at night to the villages, and we didn't carry weapons with us like other soldiers. We went to the villages in pairs; an army truck would take us from Beer-Sheba to the village and return a few hours later to pick us up. But at almost nineteen, I had the illusion that I was immortal. Doesn't everyone at this age?

About two months later, Zaki, my partner, was ill. And without him, my commanding officer flatly refused to let me go alone to the village.

"You know the rules," he said. "It's out of the question. It's against regulations."

"Then come with me," I said.

"You're forgetting yourself, Corporal. Besides, there is an officers' meeting this evening, which makes it impossible for me to go with you. And," he said, "I have no one else to spare. All the instructors are busy. Sorry." He turned to go.

But I refused to take no for an answer. "Nothing bad can happen to me," I argued. "I am familiar with the desert, and I love the desert. I know it like the palm of my hand,—so what's the big deal?" I nagged and nagged until finally he gave in with a loud sigh.

"If anyone can handle the desert, it's you, Corporal Liat Erez. Now go, I see the truck is ready to leave. Go."

Even now, I see him standing there, a neat small man looking at me with his eyebrows raised, his mouth a little open as if he were going to say more. But the truck, with me on it, took off, obscuring him in a vortex of gray dust.

During that evening's training session, the boys were strangely silent, but I noticed some peculiar hand movements that looked like secret signals. Quick flashes of eyes darted all around me. Suddenly the night seemed to be filled with whispers. I felt it closing in on me. It was spooky. My nerves were on edge. I asked Emil what was going on, but he merely looked at me and shrugged. Knowing Emil, I left it at that. We finished training early, and I decided to take a short walk by myself. I remember feeling agitated, my nerves still on edge. I wanted to be alone. I would meet the truck on its way to the village. But when I told this to Emil, he protested.

"You're not going alone," he said, suddenly looking grim, almost angry. "Wait until they come to get you."

I laughed and told him not to give me orders and not to worry. "I can take care of myself," I said. "And besides, I'm only going a little way to meet the truck."

He gazed at me in a sort of sulky silence. I noticed a muscle twitching in his cheek.

"You're worried about something," I said.

"Not at all," he said. "I just don't think it's a good idea."

I wondered and was about to change my mind to please him. I didn't.

"You're always so nervous," I said. I left him standing there, scratching his head, and looking somewhat miserable.

The night was perfect—the desert waiting, everything present in place, silent—beckoning to me, pulling me like a magnet toward its secrets; the desert haunted my mind. And although the moon was only a half-moon, it was very bright outside, like a white night, almost as bright as day but much softer. You know, one of those nights when the Milky Way flows all around you, and you feel as if you are walking, almost floating inside it, touching the stars with the tips of your fingers.

And yet, it would be a lie to say that I wasn't affected by my last exchange with Emil, and for a time, his eyes walked in front of me like two black guards.

Suddenly the silence cracked. I heard voices and turned. I saw four young men walking a little distance behind me. At first, I wasn't particularly alarmed because most people from around there knew me. Then I became aware of a mild sense of panic and began to walk faster. And when the boys caught up with me, one of them grabbed my arm while another put his hand on the nape of my neck.

"Little girl," he purred.

My heart began to palpitate and I broke out in sweat. I said to myself, Stay cool, Liat. Stay cool. And I said to them, "Hey, guys, what's going on? Who are your instructors? What village are you from?"

But they only laughed and began to push and pull me between them, while the other two stood watching grinning like two hyenas. Then one of them said, "She's this big shot, Liat. She works with Emil's group. Let's show Emil who's the king in this desert."

And I said with as much authority and coolness as I could summon at that moment, "Cut it out if you know what's good for you." But my words, useless, sounded hollow. The boys only continued to laugh, pinching my cheeks, pulling my hair, while they made strange clicking noises in their throats. Then one of them got hold of my hair from behind and yanked with such force I thought my neck would snap. He glued a garlic-smelling kiss on my lips and that made me see red, and my adrenaline shot up. I began to fight, and I knew how because it was part of my training. I was fast; that's the advantage of being small and light. But soon I was on the ground, fighting against what seemed to me thousands of hands and legs and lips. And the night didn't seem so bright anymore with my arms pinned to my side and a menacing face looming above me. I sunk my teeth into hard flesh, and a sharp, sweetish taste filled my mouth. I spat. A boy slapped my face. Someone laughed while someone else was fumbling with my belt buckle. I kicked hard. Someone screamed. A hand was clamped over my mouth, and the world became dark.

Then someone said, "I hear something. Let's get out of here. Hurry."

And the Milky Way became clear again. I stood up trembling with rage, not even bothering to wipe the dirt and blood from my face. I thought of running after them. And then what? I stood there and screamed, "Bastards! You rotten bastards! Just wait."

Suddenly I heard a high whistle and Emil's voice shouting, "They went the other way! Quick, get them!" And Didi's voice echoed, "Get them, get them."

"Emil!" I called. "Wait!"

He halted abruptly, then turned and saw me.

"Get them!" he yelled to the other boys.

"No!" I yelled.

"Go!" he yelled.

The boys ran. Only Didi waited. Emil ran toward me.

I ran after the boys, shouting, "Come back. Don't start anything. You'll get us in trouble. Come back! Come back! It's an order!" But they were oblivious to my existence. Emil caught up with me. He gripped my arm.

"Don't interfere," he said through clenched teeth. "You shouldn't be here. What happened to your face and your clothes? You're a mess. What the hell! Where's the truck?" I saw his face flush, and his eyes became almost insane with anger.

"Obviously, the truck is late," I said, trying to sound nonchalant. "And besides, you're hurting my arm, let—" But he was looking at me wildly from under dusty curls with eyes narrowed like two black cracks, and he was panting like a dog on a hot day. I saw that his face became very pale, and I felt again that sweet pain between my throat and stomach that grabbed me every time I looked at him. And for a second, our bodies came in close contact, and his breath hit me in the face, and his mouth came down on mine. It was as if for a split second, we were completely alone, until he let go of my lips. We stepped back from one another, and he cleared his throat and said, "Stay here. It's not your fight." And his voice sounded hollow and dark.

"Emil!" someone called.

"Coming!" And he ran.

I ran after him, shouting, "Emil, don't." And I heard my voice as a whisper and saw the boys holding razors in their hands, and they hissed, whistled, and circled one another like gladiators, and they kept tripping over each other and falling in a tangle then jumping up and circling and whistling and hissing again. I could hardly tell who was who and tried not to lose sight of Emil—he alone mattered. Emil was the tallest among the completely mad bunch, and Didi was jumping at his side like a mad thing in the night. And it was awful, truly awful and yet, at the same time, terribly exciting. I too wanted to join the fight and abandon myself to some primordial instinct, some primitive calling. I too wanted to bite and hit and kick and hiss, even cut, and feel and smell the sweat of those crazed bodies. I kept moving in and out of those confusing yet mesmerizing feelings, like in a dream where nothing is real, yet all is so vivid. It was incredible. I saw Emil, he was dark and predatory, and his eyes were narrowed and cold and reflected the light of the stars. And his lips were curled slightly away from his teeth in a savage smile, and Didi was dancing around him, shrieking and lisping and laughing. Then I saw Emil pull out a knife. I leaped into the air, grabbed his raised hand, and jerked at it with all my strength, and the knife fell to the ground.

I heard Emil shout, "Liat, stay back!" And Didi echoed, "Stay back, stay back."

I screamed, "Emil, look out!" and threw myself on the ground to get the knife when suddenly I felt a sharp pain, and I knew that someone had slashed my leg.

I saw my commanding officer running toward me.

I grinned at him stupidly and said, "I'm all right."

He didn't say a word, but his hands shook as he bandaged my leg.

"I am sorry," I said.

"Shut up, Liat," he said. "Just shut up."

And I did.

I saw that the four other soldiers attended to the boys from other villages that came with my commanding officer, I saw Emil standing a few feet away, staring at the sky, and I watched the excitement still burning in his eyes and the savage smile still splitting his mouth. And near Emil, gazing at him stood Didi. He was holding a hand to his right ear, and blood was oozing through his fingers. And then I heard my commanding officer say that we were all under arrest. The devil took hold of me, I began to laugh, and my laugh sounded terrible.

My commanding officer slapped my face twice and said, "Take hold of yourself, Corporal." And with tears welling in my eyes, I slowly returned to my senses, to the hellish heat, and to reality. I swallowed and didn't cry.

In the truck on the way to Beer-Sheba, Emil sat between Didi and me. Didi's ear was taped, and he was moaning softly, his eyes never leaving Emil's face and Emil's right arm around his shoulder. The boys sat among the four soldiers, expressionless. I was grateful that my commanding officer was driving because I couldn't have faced him at that moment. My eyes followed the withered thistles on each side of the dusty road, and my spirit felt withered too. Once my excitement was gone, I felt so ashamed, and utterly depleted.

At first, Emil wouldn't look at me. And when he finally did, I saw that the extraordinary wildness had left his face, and his eyes had a gloomy, cold expression. He said, "You enjoyed the fight." It was a statement, not a question. I nodded my head and turned my face away from him so he wouldn't see my tears. After a while, his mouth relaxed into a slow smile, and he looked at me with his familiar look of teasing affection. He said that when he had realized that I wasn't going to wait for the truck, he didn't know what to do because they had gotten into a quarrel with another group and were going to meet that night to "settle things" as he put it.

"How could you do this to me?" I said. "Why didn't you tell me?"

He laughed a harsh short laugh and said, "You must be joking. It was very stupid of you to walk by yourself. You got us all in trouble, and now they'll send you away to do something safe, and they won't even let you say good-bye to us."

"You shouldn't have pulled that knife," I said.

He looked at me, and his eyes narrowed, and he gave a short snort. "Don't be so dumb," he said. "If I hadn't pulled out the knife, you could have kissed this whole rotten world good-bye forever."

And that shut me up. For a while, we sat there swaying to the bouncing of the truck, avoiding each other's eyes. He stared out at the moonlit desert, and I could see that under his anger was a layer of coldness and an unforgiving distance he had placed between us.

"You're terribly naive about life, Commander Liat," he said. "It's time you grow up because the world isn't as you imagine it to be—wonderful—and," he said wistfully, "it'll do you good to learn the facts of real life." He kept glancing at the bloodstained bandage on my leg, and I saw him clench his left hand. In his eyes, I saw something of fear or maybe of shame, but probably I only imagined it.

"It's nothing," I said. "It doesn't hurt at all."

"Yah, sure," he said.

I saw he didn't believe me, and I had no words to comfort him. I squeezed his hand and noticed his face soften. He looked at me, and I felt as if he were looking into the most secret place in me. For only a second, I felt his hand close on mine; then he pulled his hand away and lowered his eyes. It was as if the entrance to his soul had closed forever. A sense of a terrible loss came over me; I wanted to weep from shame, frustration, and love. At that moment, it seemed that everything important in my life was gone. It felt like in a dream, when the heart strains and you want to scream but you can't utter a sound. I didn't weep because I was Commander Liat, a soldier in the IDF; but at that moment, this thought made me so sick that I hung over the side of the truck and vomited, terrified that the boys would laugh at me. No one even smiled.

When we reached Beer-Sheba, we were taken to the army hospital where they had cleaned out the cuts on my face, stitched and bandaged my leg, and let me go. But I was confined to my room until a decision was reached about me. For three days I lay on my bed and stared at the ceiling and thought of Emil. Sometimes I would fall into semi-sleep, and my sleep would be infested with dreams of pits and crawling things, and I would wake up sweating, my heart palpitating. And at night, unable to sleep, I'd stand by the open window and gaze at the desert's stars and sniff the desert odors of faraway bonfires and hot dust and think of special moments I had shared with Emil like the night we smoked the hashish, that night when Zaki took the boys for a special night training session. Emil had complained of a migraine headache, and so he and I stayed behind. We sat very close without touching, without words, and watched as the moon. Emil was smoking. After a while, he said, "Here, take a puff."

"I don't smoke," I said, "and you shouldn't either. I thought you have a headache."

But he merely laughed and said, "Try, it won't kill you." His voice was hoarse, and his mouth seemed very dry. I took the peculiar-shaped cigarette, inhaled, and almost choked; but Emil didn't laugh.

"I want you," he said, but he didn't move. I had no idea what was going to happen next. I felt strange, not unpleasant, as if I am detached from myself and very quiet inside. I talked with an effort because my tongue felt somewhat paralyzed.

"I don't think it's a good idea. It will ruin everything."

He didn't answer. He only reached out, took my hands, and held them in his, but he didn't make love to me. I sat very still. But he only continued to hold my hands and gaze at me with his eyes half closed, a kind of vacant smile on his face. And that was all we did: looking at each other, smiling, dreaming, and holding hands—probably looked utterly ridiculous.

Near Tel Aviv, a few months later, I was sitting at my open window, feeling the sea breeze caress my face, breathing the perfume of apple blossoms, watching the night sky above my head. Suddenly the telephone rang. I got up annoyed and a little frightened. Who could it be at such an ungodly hour? I picked up the phone expecting anyone but the voice of my commander.

"Liat?" he said.

"Gideon?" I said.

"I have bad news."

I sat down on the bed.

"Liat, are you there?"

"Where are you?"

"In Beersheba."

"Tell me."

He was silent.

"Gideon, talk to me."

"Emil was rejected by the army. The medical examiner said that he has a mental disorder. At eight o'clock this morning, he shot himself in the head with his brother's gun. He died instantly."

Silence.

"Liat?"

"Yes."

"The funeral is tomorrow at four in the afternoon. Shall I pick you up?"

"Gideon."

"Yes?"

"Thanks. But . . ."

I hung up the phone, went back to the window, and looked up at the sky. I thought about Emil and how,—for only one moment—I felt his heart drumming on my breasts, how his mouth tasted, how it was to smoke hashish. Then I went into the room, sat on the floor, and stared at the darkness. My eyes were dry, but I couldn't breathe. I didn't go to the funeral. After three days, Gideon came; and when he took me in his arms, I began to scream, and I screamed and screamed. And Gideon just held me without saying a word. What was there to say? Emil's death was empty of reason as can be, and I had never even told him how much I wanted him. One wouldn't believe things like that are possible, but it was possible then, and for Emil, perhaps it was the only way.

For a long time, Liat and Pauline sit in silence. Liat's eyes are closed, her breathing shallow. Her entire stormy life is etched on her face. Pauline knows that Liat doesn't expect her to say anything.

The painting is now complete in her mind. She knows.

Suddenly both women jump. Liat's closed eyes spring open; her hand flies to her heart. "My god!" she exclaims. "Your doorbell! Who can it be at this hour?"

"I have no idea," says Pauline.

The doorbell rings again.

Pauline gets up, goes to the door, and looks through the peephole.

She feels her pulse quicken. She opens the door.

"Hello, Pauline," says Philip.

"Philip!" Liat cries. "How did you know I was here?" And to Pauline's surprise, she runs to him, hugs his waist, and presses her cheek into his chest. And he, with his huge palm, strokes her short black hair like one strokes a little child. They stand like that for a time. Philip looks over Liat's head straight at Pauline and shakes his head; his forehead wrinkles in anxiety. Liat turns her head and smiles. "Good-bye, Pauline," she says. Embarrassed, she adds, "Thanks."

That night, Pauline finishes the painting.

The exhibition was a great success. Everyone wanted to know who is the girl in the painting, and the dark boy, and the half-lion half-man who crouches in the distance, watching them through half-closed eyes.

"Just people I know," says Pauline.

She walks around the gallery, talks to the guests, and smiles and smiles and smiles. She feels as if her face is cracking.

Someone taps her on the shoulder. Startled, she whirls around.

"Big success," says Philip.

"Thank you." Pauline's heart beats with unusual force. Her hands perspire.

"How much?" Philip asks. "How much do you want for the painting?"

"The painting is not for sale," Pauline whispers.

"The desert," Philip says. "Liat went back to the desert; to its odors of bonfires and burnt thorns, its white nights and hot gray dust; 'to its silence,' as she said it. I begged her to let me come with her. She refused. 'I can't run away any longer,' she said. 'The images are haunting me.' I had no idea what she meant. And when I insisted to come with her, she cried, 'No, Philip, don't you understand? I have to do this alone!' I asked when she'd be back. She shook her head. 'I'm so sorry, Philip,' she said. 'So sorry.' And when I said, 'I'm your husband, what about me?' she said, 'what about you, Philip? You're a strong man. You'll get over me.'"

Philip looks at the floor. Pauline knows he's embarrassed. He said too much. She watches as he rubs his temples. She wants to put her arms around his neck. She wants to caress his graying hair. Instead she says, "Be patient. Liat will be back."

He looks at her for a long moment then reaches out a hand and very lightly touches her cheek. "Your eyes are red," he says. "You need sleep."

She is unable to read his face. She wants to say something consoling, soothing. She watches him walk away. Pauline closes her eyes for a moment and takes a deep breath; then fixing the smile on her face, she turns back to her guests.

The next day she sends the painting to Philip.

A few days later, Pauline receives a short note:

I told you that everything worth painting had already been painted. It seems I was wrong. I will pick you up at eight.

Thanks.

Philip

BLUEBIRD

She disappeared into the fog
my bluebird.
At night I watch cold, scolding stars
by day I lift a hoping face
toward a granite sky
that devours my eyes with bitter mists.

She vanished like my youth,
and I had not a clue to how or when
or where the days had passed
melted dumbly like morning dew
becoming shadows
on the walls of my
youth.

Fierce were my days
passionate my loves
I wove a tapestry of life
my spirit blossomed then
like buds in spring.
Where has it gone, the life
fled without a sign,
I see my image erased
inside indifferent eyes
of a proud generation
that cannot even cry.

And still I wait
for the mists to lift
and still I stare
into unyielding sky
whistling, calling, begging:
come back, Bluebird
sing again for me
I am not ready to
let go of
the light.

ILANA HALEY

FACE-LIFT

He opens the door wide
offers her a mustached smile
and utters in an oily voice,
"You're so beautiful."

The wrinkles on her face deepen
her eyes sink in their sockets
the skin of her neck crumples
the spots on her hands darken.

He sits in the black leather chair
she perches on the royal blue couch
in one hand he holds a glass of white wine
she clutches a tiny mirror to her chest
between his lips trembles a cigarette
she stares at the brown spots on her naked arm
(the oil paintings on his walls are terrific)
he laughs, he roars
he continues to seduce:
words, words, words,
pecking at her like ravens' shrieks.

And though he is her friend
of many years
she does not believe him
because his eyes are dead
his face opaque
his fingers shake—
the wine crumbles his brain.

And she, she only sees how
with the downing of each young morn
her beauty drowns
into the depth of the
looking glass.

HEART BARK

It is morning
the devils of the night
are gone.
I lay in my bed
waiting for him
to enter my room
and gather me
to his heart,
his body exuding
scent of night,
and he'll whisper
"My love, my one and only love."
But perhaps not,
perhaps he will forget,
forget me like my father did,
when he left and
joined the dead.

He entered my room
and climbed into my bed
and clasped his hands under
his head and stared at the ceiling
and sighed.
He did not say My Love,
we did not make love,
he only heaved another sigh
then got up
and left.

I leaped from the bed
and screamed,
"Good morning, world!"
The neighbor's dog answered
my greeting
in a nasty bark.

HIS DAUGHTER

She cringed and crawled inside herself
as she observed the feverish veil of expectation
darkening his eyes.
She did not want to hear the words
that jailed her spirit with a gentle fist of love,
as he placed his lust for fame
upon her tender shoulders, so very young.
She saw the weird excitement twist his
handsome mouth as he dreamed aloud
the glory of her future life:
"Look at the neon lights," he said,
"One day they'll scream your name."
But the light in his eyes was sucked inside,
pulsating through the secret chambers of his heart.
In every neon light, he saw her name,
each throbbing burst of light
proclaimed his name with fervent adoration.
And she, his little daughter
shivered, bent, almost broke,
under the strangling yoke of love
he placed upon her heart,
when, with cheeks aglow and
restless eyes, he told her
of the life of fame he dreams for her,
his little gem,
his genius of
a daughter.

DON'T TOUCH ME

Don't touch me just now,
a dead man lies in my arms,
the mirrors are veiled,
the candles smolder,
and weeping is not yet welcome.

Don't touch me just now,
with eyes of night I am staring,
embracing his body with quivering arms
for the earth is cold, frost stiffens the grass
and all from the beginning is fixed as law.

Don't touch me just now, go,
come back with the wind, tomorrow
this man will be here no more,
desolation lies
in my arms.

TOUCH ME

Touch, now, my body
That rejuvenates with the morning,
Submerges with the evening
And consumes into the night.
There isn't another place
Except here, in our congested home
Among the dust hugging its walls,
The dust of our love, almost diaphanous,
Still quivering to the touch of light,
Engulfing us with longing
To a place that belongs
Only to you
And me.

THE ROSES ARE DYING

(MAYA)

They were taking a drive one Saturday in early fall when the countryside was beautifully deserted, untainted by the presence of man; and the air was still without a hint of wind, full of birds singing; and the smell of falling leaves rose from the ground. Far above the tops of the trees, she could see the trail of a jet stream. The sun's rays penetrated the outstretched branches like silver arrows, but the serenity of her surrounding only intensified her disquiet.

How silent she is, Eric thought. She was staring straight ahead, her face drawn, and he noticed the perspiration on her forehead. He reached for her hand. It was damp, and her fingers were trembling. He let her be and continued to drive slowly through the gold-speckled afternoon. But as time passed and she still didn't say a word, he felt himself becoming restless. It wasn't fun for him. He wanted her laughing, talking, loving. Instead, she had been edging away since he'd picked her up. But it wasn't only today. Lately, she had been self-absorbed, anxious. He had wanted to tell her something very important for some time, but her bleak moods had held him back.

He pulled the car to a stop and absently watched the scattered leaves, waiting for her to speak to him.

She remained silent.

"What's bothering you?" he finally asked.

"Don't stare at me," she whispered, turning away from him.

"I've never seen you act so strange."

He took her hands, but she withdrew them.

"For heaven's sake, Maya, what is it?"

"He wants to have a baby."

He had to struggle to prevent himself from taking her by the shoulders and shaking her.

"Look at me, Maya. I can't hear you."

She turned to him. "Jason insists on having a baby."

He lit a cigarette and inhaled greedily.

"You are his wife." He blew a jet of smoke. "It's natural for a husband to want to have a child with his wife."

"You don't understand," she flared. "I don't love Jason."

"What a romantic you are," he smiled. I'll tell her now, he decided. "It would be lovely to have a child with you," he said, his voice slightly husky.

"What!"

"Maya, relax." He took her into his arms.

She disengaged herself.

"Come on, don't be so melodramatic," he said irritably. "When a man wants to have a child with a woman, it's not an insult. It means he loves her." He took a deep breath. "Almost since I met you, I have thought that I'd like to have a child with you. And now that Jason wants the same thing, it should be easy."

"Are you mad?"

"Maya," he pleaded, "don't you get it? Jason will think it's his child. No one will know until we can be married."

"Married? And when would that happen? We've never even talked of it."

"It will happen, it will happen."

She put up her hand. "Stop it, Eric. Be quiet."

They sat there as silent as the bright afternoon.

He would never leave his wife and daughters, she thought. It didn't matter. She didn't want to marry him. She wanted to leave Jason, but she didn't want to marry Eric or anyone else.

She could have a boy, Eric was thinking. He loved his three daughters, but he badly wanted a boy. A son would be wonderful. She mustn't leave Jason now. He looked at her, all tense and anxious, and remembered a different time with her:

It was night. Snow-covered mountains surrounded them. The sky was luminous, full of shining stars.

"I see a building," she said.

He laughed.

"It's like a dream. Where are we?"

"We are lost in the snow." He laughed again.

Just then, they entered the village. Like a vision, it appeared before them encircled by giant mountains, like something out of a children's book. The mountains, brilliant with snow, seemed almost transparent under the stars. Mountains were his passion. They represented all his dreams of mystery, beauty, and power. In their presence, he became enchanted by the limitlessness of his possibilities, his freedom. They infused him with strength; and yet, confronted by their immortality, he felt humbled. He looked at her standing beside him, her eyes reflecting the flickering lights. Her face under her white fur hat seemed suspended in the whiteness of the mountains. He was filled with sudden, deep happiness. It was at that moment that he first knew he wanted to have a child with her. A son. The idea had been in his mind almost from the moment he had met her a year earlier, but this was the first time he experienced the full force of it, of his love for her. Surrounded by his beloved mountains where he felt most alive, he felt the pulse of his life flowing freely, and he longed to become one with the mountains and one with her.

"Eric," she said, "I can't breathe."

He laughed and took her in his arms. "It's the high altitude. It will pass."

"I hope so," she said, gasping for breath.

But he was oblivious to all except to the reflection of his dream on her face.

The next morning, he took her by the lift to the top. His territory. They stood together in the middle of nowhere, in the middle of everywhere, and shouted as loud as they could. He shouted her name, she his; their voices bounced from mountain to mountain. Holding tightly to one another, they rolled in the snow.

"I want to make love to you here," he said. Excitement filled his body. She laughed and rolled away. He came after her fast and pulled her down with him. They lay in the snow. His face above her blocked the sun, and the stillness seemed forever.

His mountains. His Maya.

"Let's go back," he heard her say now.

"What? I want to make love to you," he said, still high on his mountains, dreamily caressing the wisps of black hair that fell on her face.

She smoothed her hair back impatiently. "So does Jason. Take me home, Eric!"

He was surprised at the harshness of her tone.

"Maya," he said, "don't you remember the mountains?"

She lowered her eyes. "Of course I remember the mountains," she said, "how could I forget? Take me home now, Eric."

He saw the effort she was making to hold back tears. It's all right, he thought. She needs time to adjust. He had no doubt she would.

In the days that followed, Maya examined her feelings frantically. Did she want Eric's child? She knew of his desire for a boy. Jason's too. How vulnerable men are, she thought. Could the fear of obliteration be so strong within a man? Jason continued to press her. "Now is the time, while we are young, Maya." And Eric was saying, "Have a baby with me, a child of love, Maya!" She didn't expect anything from Eric. He was married, selfish, and mad. She loved him from the moment she met him, perhaps despite Jason, maybe because of Jason.

She hoped to become a great ballerina and had been devoting her life to this goal. But after excruciating years of hard, daily work, she slowly began to realize that she would never be great. The thought of being a mediocre ballerina was repulsive to her; settling for second best was not part of her nature. But she hadn't been ready to give up. She forgot to eat, she couldn't sleep she only danced and danced. Until one day, during a performance, she collapsed from total exhaustion.

It was a year earlier, at a New Year's party, that she had met Jason. He was very tall,—almost a giant. His eyes behind their thick lenses were enormous and slightly out of focus. His face was long and pale, its expression solemn. He neither drank nor danced, his whole being screamed of solitude. Clearly, he didn't belong at the party, but then neither did she. She was glad that he didn't want to dance because her feet still throbbed from the night's performance. They found an empty dimly lit room, sat on the bare floor, and talked until the small hours. She talked; he mostly listened. She liked him. He fell madly in love with her.

After that night, they saw each other often. He would meet her after the ballet, bring her flowers, take her to dinner; but what she loved the best was to sit in his garden and talk or just be quiet and watch the flowers bloom and the butterflies flutter among the ferns.

A month later, he asked her to marry him. She laughed and said, "I'm already married."

"Can't you marry me too?" He didn't laugh. He didn't even smile.

"No," she said.

She continued to see him, and he continued to ask her to marry him. "I won't interfere with the ballet," he would promise.

She thought about it. She felt safe and peaceful with him, but she didn't love him, not the way she loved the ballet,—a love that took her breath away and kept her floating, soaring.

After her collapse on the stage, Jason came to see her in her apartment every day. "Marry me, Maya." He was a most persistent man.

It was during those ten days, when she lay in her bed exhausted and depressed, that she decided to leave the ballet. And she did.

Three months later, she married Jason. He loved her with passion and tenderness, which made her feel ashamed. She tried very hard to be a good wife, and he never complained, not even about her reluctance to make love.

Jason was away on business a great deal of the time. Maya spent most of her days in their gardens: pruning, grooming, planting flowers and shrubs. But more often than not, she sat quietly, watching the roses,—tall and elegant,—swaying in the summer breeze, her mind focused on a time she had moved with as subtle a grace.

It was late evening, and Jason was away on one of his trips. She sat in her garden, leafing abstractedly through the paper, when suddenly the words struck her: the Bolshoi was in town. She jumped off her chair. She mustn't miss the performance, but a glance at her watch told her she was probably too late. Besides, it was unlikely she'd get a ticket. Nonetheless, dressed in her jeans and sweatshirt, her hair disheveled, her face smeared with earth, she ran to the street and jumped into a taxi. When she arrived at the theater, the doors were already shut. Then she saw a man running toward a closed door. She saw that he held two tickets in his hand. She ran, caught up with him, and asked if he had an extra ticket. Hardly looking at her, he grabbed her hand. "Come on," he said, pulling her inside with him; and before she knew it, she was sitting in one of the best seats in the house, watching her favorite ballet. *The dream* was upon her again, and she abandoned herself to the fantasy that she had been cut from time and place and became Odette.

She had forgotten all about the man sitting next to her, but later in the performance, she became aware of his presence. And inside her dream of gliding beauty, she felt her hand in his. She tried to pull her hand away, but his grip was strong. She turned her head and looked at him. His face was tanned, a little weathered; his gray eyes had a mischievous glint. She thought him the most attractive man she had ever seen. He smiled. "My name is Eric," he whispered. He wet his thumb with saliva and rubbed at her cheek. "You have mud on your face." His lips touched her ear; she shuddered. And suddenly, incredibly, the dancers receded, became pale and distant as phantoms, and then ceased to exist. She saw only him.

"Let's go," he said and took her hand again, pulling her off her seat. It was overwhelmingly physical, something she had never in her life thought possible. She became his obsession; he became her ballet.

For over two years, she had shared her life with two men; and now pressured by each to have his child, she was assaulted by chaos. She felt she was swaying on a trembling foundation. She was adored by two men; but adoration, she knew, was like a drug,—too powerful to resist and dangerous.

Fall vanished, the icy winter fled, and spring came with its illusion of promise. "You'd love having a baby, Maya," Jason would say.

"A child of love, Maya," Eric whispered, his lips hovering on hers, his eyes promising paradise.

And Maya began to see herself with an infant in her arms. Her baby.

They lay entwined. How beautiful Eric's body was; its sensation lingered in the flesh of her arms and thighs. But to her surprise, she could not abandon herself completely to his love. Her body felt shut. She didn't think that he was aware of her lack of passion; but after a brief sleep, he opened his eyes, propped himself up on his elbow, and lit a cigarette. "Were are you, Maya? Were you thinking of Jason?"

"No, she said, and indeed she wasn't thinking of Jason. She kissed his lips lightly, and smiling to herself, she jumped off the bed and began to dress.

He put out the cigarette and sat up. "Where are you going?" he asked.

"Home. I need to think."

"Think here." She heard the impatience in his voice.

"I need to be alone."

"You always need to be alone."

She turned to him. "I don't want to have a child, Eric, and I have decided I'm not going to. It would be crazy for me to gratify the narcissistic wish of yours. Crazy. So forget it."

"And what will you tell Jason?" His voice sharpened.

"I don't have to tell him anything," she threw at him." And anyway, Eric, you're forgetting that he is my husband."

"You always remind me," he threw back at her.

"Let's not fight," she said, and all the frustration and pain that darkened her life since she left the ballet flowed again into her voice, poisoning the air of love, she was breathing only a few minutes before.

His eyes narrowed. "You're not going anywhere," he said as, with a swift motion, he grabbed her and pulled her, half-dressed, onto the bed. You don't want my child?" His face was red. His lips bit into her lips. He was in such a fever of rage and desire that it frightened her.

"Let go!" She tried to get out from underneath him, but his furious embrace was like a vise. How desperately he needed to prove that she belonged to him. Suddenly, involuntarily, she laughed an abrupt laugh. Startled, she turned her head and looked at him. His eyes were ablaze with the same excitement she had seen in his face on the mountain.

"No," she said, but her eyes wavered. She turned away, but he forced her head back.

"It'll be my boy!"

The density of emotion with which he said those words made her skin tingle. Again, overwhelmingly, she felt the force that tied her to this man. Her resistance collapsed, and in spite of herself, she felt a stirring deep inside her. Her body gave in, then her mind, and she abandoned herself to his passion and her own.

Her pain eased, and she opened her eyes. The enormous white light above her head threatened to drink her up. She had been in labor for many hours. It would not have been so awful had she known that her baby was alive. But she was sure that the baby inside her was dead. Her pain returned with terrifying speed. Her teeth began to chatter. Her head reeled, and her whole body was ablaze with fever. She heard someone screaming. She felt a prick of a needle and lost consciousness.

When she came to, the pain seemed distant, but as she increasingly became aware of her surroundings, she realized that she was no longer alone. There seemed to be a lot happening between her strapped legs. Eyes hung above her. Masks swayed dangerously. Voices jabbed her.

"Push hard, Maya. Harder!" The voice scraped at Maya's exposed nerves. She shut her eyes and pushed with all her might. Waves of nausea assaulted her. She twisted her right arm from its strap and hit the nurse's thigh. *Let me out of here.* But the words, as in a dream, were merely an echo in her mind.

The nurse forced Maya's hand back into the strap. "How did she manage to free her arm?"

Another nurse rushed to assist. "Try to relax," she said to Maya and patted her hand.

She heard the doctor command, "Push harder!" She felt him sitting on her belly.

"Push! Push! Push!" The doctor's voice was angry. Maya summoned all that was left of her strength, held her breath, and with a desperate effort, pushed until she felt the veins on her neck ready to tear. She felt her flesh ripping. She fainted.

As she came to, she heard the nurse complaining, "Jesus, my feet are killing me."

"She is having a hard time," the other nurse said. She dabbed Maya's bleeding lips with ice.

"They all have a hard time," the first nurse replied crossly. Then more softly, she added, "But this one is having it real bad. And all for a dead baby."

"Shah. She might hear you. Don't talk so loud."

"She can't hear me. She's out of it, lucky for her."

My name is Maya Margolis! Maya screamed in her mind.

The doctor bent his face over her and said, "He's dead. I'm sorry."

"Fuck you!" she shouted and felt triumphant because the words finally broke out of her throat. She heard the nurse giggle and the embarrassed laugh of the doctor. She didn't even know his name. Her triumph collapsed. She felt abused, betrayed.

The doctor said, "You can put her out now."

"No! No!" She made an effort to sit up. A hand pushed her back down; and as the mask was placed on her face, she wondered, why are they killing me now?"

Dusky light poured through the tall window and fell on the narrow bed. On the white wall opposite, a painting of Jesus, his head falling limply to his right shoulder, hung crookedly above a table loaded with white roses. There were roses everywhere. The air in the room was dense, their heavy fragrance overlaying the odors of disinfectants and drugs. A nun finished arranging the flowers. She walked silently to the bed and looked at Maya's motionless body. She crossed herself quickly, tucked the blankets around her patient, and smiled reassuringly at the visitor who was seated by the bed, staring fixedly at the woman's sleeping face. "Don't stay too long. She needs rest," the nun said and left the room.

The visitor was not even aware of her departure; so intent was he on Maya. He would have liked to touch her hair but couldn't bring himself to do so.

He waited. He had been waiting there since they took Maya to the delivery room at seven in the morning. He had wanted to go with her to the delivery room, but the nurse would not let him. "It's going to be a difficult delivery, Mr. Margolis. We're not sure we can save the baby."

"What about Maya? Is she going to be all right?"

"She'll be fine," the nurse reassured him.

But he wasn't convinced. "Where is the doctor?" he demanded.

"Who is her doctor?"

"Dr. Baker."

"Dr. Baker is away. The attending physician is Dr. Kline."

"But she doesn't know him. She'll be terribly upset."

"This is an emergency, Mr. Margolis, and in emergencies like this, the doctor on duty takes over. Dr. Kline is a fine doctor."

"I would like to talk to Dr. Kline." Jason thought he would convince the doctor to let him see Maya. But before he had a chance to ask, the doctor said, "Mr. Margolis, it's better if you wait outside." When Jason began to protest, the doctor snapped, "We're very busy here. You're in the way." And he closed the door in Jason's face.

"Bastard," Jason said under his breath. "Bastard bastard bastard," he repeated as he walked back to Maya's room to wait.

Maya wasn't brought down until four in the afternoon. Even then, she was still unconscious. She looked so small, childlike. He could see the veins on her hands and neck, and the faint pulse of her throat. He stared at her bleeding lips. He was to blame. She hadn't wanted a baby. He convinced her to have a child. At first, she reacted so fiercely that it scared him. How had she changed?

She had always been a little reserved, dreamy. Not being of a demonstrative nature himself, he had liked her that way. But now she was unreachable, and at times even hostile. Was she in love with another man? He asked her no questions. Was he afraid of what he might discover? She didn't even want to play their private game anymore. When he met her, she had told him that she loved roses, especially white roses; when he returned from a trip, he always brought her white roses. "Oh, Jason, how lovely," she would smile. She would arrange the roses in a clay vase; then she would climb up on the sofa or on a chair and, laughing, put her arms around his neck and embrace him. It was a sort of joke between them, he being so tall that she only reached his chest. But lately she seemed indifferent to his homecoming; ignoring the roses, he never failed to bring her.

He remembered one summer evening in particular:

They were sitting in their garden. The sun had set, leaving the sky clear, with a trace of evening red in it. He had just returned from London. He was sipping a glass of wine, watching the fireflies dance among the flowers, and quietly listened to the sound of the crickets. She sat on a lounge chair, hugging her knees to her chest, gazing into the dark. There it was again, this look in her eyes that seemed to exclude him completely. He wondered what she was thinking. After a while, he got up and sat next to her on the lounge chair.

"You're so lovely tonight, Maya," he said. His finger caressed the nape of her neck. He looked at her face, and the desire to have a child with her overwhelmed him once more. She smiled at him. He saw that her eyes were full of longing. But they didn't connect with him. It was as though she didn't really see him.

"What's the matter, Maya?"

"Why nothing."

"You seem so far away."

"It's such a lovely evening," she said as though she hadn't heard him.

"Then why are you unhappy?" His hand was still on the nape of her neck. She moved restlessly.

"Don't move away from me like this," he said. He finished his drink in one gulp, got up, and went inside to fix himself another drink. Suddenly, forgetting the wine, he took a volume of Shakespeare from the shelf and leafed through it until he found what he was looking for. He came back to the garden and sat next to her. She didn't move.

"Maya," he said, "do you remember Shakespeare's second sonnet? Listen." And he began to read the sonnet out aloud, emphasizing each word. He read in a low voice, but as he continued to read, his voice got louder until, as he concluded, it was almost a shout:

This fair child of mine
Shall sum my count and make my old excuse
Proving his beauty by succession thine
This to be new-made when thou are old
And see thy blood warm when thou feel'st it cold.

While he was reading, she sat quietly, focusing all her attention on him. When he finished, he closed the book and waited. She remained still. Only now, her face was white, and her eyes looked down at the motionless hand in her lap.

"Well, isn't it beautiful?" he asked triumphantly. "Doesn't it sum it all up perfectly?"

She reacted so fiercely that it scared him. She jumped up, her face turned red, her expression grim, and there was scorn in her voice. "Jason, this is selfish, believing that we'll live forever through our children. Your desire for a child has nothing to do with me or love." She stood glaring at him. "Jason, I—" She took a deep breath. He thought she was about to say more. He hoped she'd say more, explain her behavior. He waited, his eyes glued to her lips. "Jason, I don't," she stammered. "Oh, what's the use?" she cried then ran from the garden.

He had wanted to follow her, but he did not. He sat for a time, gazing at the rosebush. Suddenly its thorns seemed menacing. The fierceness of this attack made him sick. He couldn't understand her anger, her distance. She exasperated him, made him feel invisible.

But after several distant months, Maya told him that she was pregnant. He was ecstatic. He caught her in his arms, lifted her up, and spun her around, laughing with joy and relief. She shouted at him to let go of her. He lost his balance, almost dropped her.

During her pregnancy, Maya insisted on sleeping alone in the spare bedroom. She seemed to be living completely inside herself, but he didn't press her. He tried to console himself with the thought that it was a woman's way while expecting, that after the baby was born, things would change. She'd be happy with him, love him. He vowed to himself to be home more. He even thought of a name for the baby. Joseph, like his father.

But the nights were cold, and he couldn't get warm.

"Mr. Margolis!"

Jason looked up, startled. A nurse was beckoning to him. He hesitated. He fancied that Maya's eyelids fluttered.

"Mr. Margolis, could you step outside for a moment?" Reluctantly, he followed the nurse.

"Sit down, Mr. Margolis."

"What is it?" He didn't sit down.

The nurse said, "I'm sorry. The baby didn't make it."

"Dead," Jason moaned.

"There wasn't anything we could do," the nurse was saying. "The baby died inside of her. It was . . ."

But Jason was already in Maya's room.

Maya resisted coming back to consciousness, but she had no choice. Life's energy was plowing its way through her exhausted body and numbed mind. She opened her eyes and immediately shut them. She kept them shut, squeezing her lids tightly. A feeling of apprehension engulfed her.

She knew she must open her eyes and keep them open. Slowly she emerged, forced by the determination of her heartbeat. Her eyes cleared, and she saw the motionless figure of her observer.

It was only Jason in his gray suit, his face white with tension, the lines around his mouth so deep they looked almost black.

Eric. Where was Eric? Why wasn't Eric here? She reined in her mind.

Jason was a fact. He had to be dealt with. But Maya was not ready to deal with anything, so she remained passive; and as Jason waited for her to return to life, she waited for him to say or do whatever he would.

All she heard was Jason breathing her name. "Maya . . . Maya . . ." A mist covered his lenses. She managed a feeble smile—more like a grimace. She felt ashamed and wanted to cry. She was irritated by Jason's monumental appearance and soft voice. From such a huge frame should come a thundering voice.

"Maya, wake up. It's me." His insistent whisper was abrasive, pushing his presence upon her. She stopped resisting and looked into his eyes. He took her hand and kissed it.

"I am sorry, Jason." She withdrew her hand.

"No, Maya, don't. We'll have other children." Seeing the anxiety leap into her eyes, he paused, unsure of himself. She did not say anything. Tentatively he covered her hand with his huge palm. She moved her head restlessly; her eyes wandered around the room, flitting past the white roses, coming to rest on the picture of Jesus hanging above the white table. For a moment, she saw him, so lonely, hanging between two thieves, imagining the nails being driven into his flesh.

She turned her head back to look at Jason. His face was a blur. A gray haze moved in on her, promising to obliterate the world once more. Before she let go completely, she thought of Eric, and a bitter smile slashed the pallor of her face.

Jason was baffled. A surge of anxiety washed over him like a huge wave, leaving him shaking. He reached out a diffident hand to touch her shoulder but withdrew it immediately. He sat glumly for a long time, his hands clasped between his knees.

When finally he found the courage to take her hand and hold it, Maya did not open her eyes. She seemed to be sleeping deeply.

The phone by her bed was ringing. He picked it up quickly, not wanting her disturbed.

"Hello?" Jason whispered. No one answered. "Hello?" Jason said again. The receiver on the other end was replaced. The disconnected line buzzed at him like a hovering bee.

Jason put down the phone and looked closely at his wife. Maya was still asleep, but her fists were clenched, and a deep line was etched between her eyebrows. As Jason leaned closer, Eric's name escaped her lips. Or had he only imagined it? "Maya?" He squeezed her hand. But her eyes remained closed. "Maya, who is Eric?"

"Eric," she murmured again.

At that moment, the emptiness of the room locked around him. He let go of her hand and stood up.

The sun had set, leaving husband and wife in darkness. Jason stood looming above her. The nun came in. She turned on the light at the foot of the bed. Jason blinked. He took off his glasses and rubbed his eyes.

"Time to leave," the nun said kindly as she bent over Maya. "Your wife is fine. She'll sleep through the night." She looked at Jason, her eyes brimming with compassion. "I am sorry about your baby. But she's young, you'll have other children." She smiled serenely.

"Yes."

"Are you all right?"

"What?"

"Are you feeling okay?" She was looking at him closely.

"It's so hot in here," he said. "The roses are dying."

"You should go home and rest. It's late." She patted his arm slightly.

"It's late," he echoed. He turned away from his sleeping wife; and slowly, shuffling his feet, he left that suffocating room with its wilting white roses and the gloomy picture of the crucified Jesus, took the elevator to the lobby, and walked out of the hospital into the night.

He moved slowly along the dark avenue, disturbing thoughts invading his mind. He felt weighted down by loneliness. His eyes felt sore, his throat dry. He noticed the lights of a tavern.

He entered the tavern and walked right to the bar. He ordered a double scotch. He was halfway through his third drink when someone tapped him on his shoulder. Neil Dunbar raised his slight body onto the next stool and stuck out his hand. "Jason!" he exclaimed, his kind face beaming. "Well, what is it, a boy or a girl?"

Jason stared at his friend, his eyes glazed with fatigue and dilated by alcohol. He didn't deliberately ignore Neil's proffered hand; he didn't see it. In a voice barely audible, he said, "I forgot to ask."

ANOTHER LOVE STORY

Today, as I passed along the street
I saw you, by chance, after many years,
sitting with yourself in a plush restaurant,
gaping at youth swaying their hips in front of you
through a glass of an empty dream.

I halted. I stared at you. But you didn't see me.
I felt my life stretching back,
becoming diaphanous
as butterflies' wings.

For years I sat in darkened rooms,
enveloped in foul cigarette smoke,
yearning, counting minutes, hours—
breaking.

And you came,
and I love you, you proclaimed,
but your eyes stared through me, lusting
after a world
outside me.

In the silent echo of my love's memory, I spoke to you:

How can you hear my silence
when you couldn't
hear my words?

How can you feel my sorrow
when you couldn't
heed my joy?

How will you hold my wrinkled hand
when you dropped
my fair one?

How will you kiss my wilted lips
when my laughing mouth
you ignored?

How will you listen, now, to the pains of my years
when to the joy of my youth
you were deaf?

Sorrow wells up in me—
Also
love.

The silken thread has unraveled.

I returned
to my loving man,
and you—
to whom
did
you
return?

SHE WAS

She was big and beautiful, her face
like forest dwellers.
Sun sparks danced in the mane of her hair,
in the soft grass of her eyes
a melody played an eternal song.

She spun life with her deft fingers,
she drank youth in breathless lust.

She did not allow the world around her to rest
"I am consumed by the fire of life,"
she would say, retreating from stillness
as from a terrible foe.

Once she said she was freezing.
She said, "I don't belong in this world,
my time has come to enter another dimension."

We smiled, embarrassed.
We said,
"You are in love with pain."
Her gaze damp and melancholic
a tiny smile crumpled her lips—
her eyes sea deep.

On a spring morning
we found her sprawled on the floor,
her veins torn, a mysterious smile of wonder
stamped on her tanned face, so dead.

For seven days and seven nights
we mourned her—
as is our custom.
And each year
I sit there
under the cypress tree
in the calm of the
Rocky Hill
listening to her voice
wafting to me in the wind,
"I am consumed by the fire of life."

VISITATION

My eyelids are transparent
you are standing on the other side of the bed

your body glimmers in the darkness
I see the white bones of your skeleton

do you remember the fish bone
that got stuck in your gullet?

you said I was happy you suffered
you were right then

it's good to see your bones
stay there, on the other side of the bed

you smell of tunnels
you smell of too much time

you settle on me like age
you descend on me like dust

trapped inside myself
I shout

Let me out

you belong to

another dimension

you can't.

TOUCH HIM

Touch him
don't
You see
He is oozing
Bless him
don't
You see
He's breaking

Smile at him
Speak love to him
Kiss his head
Forgive him
Now
Don't you see
He is saying
Good-bye.

YOU

You came in the dark
and took my hand
and led me a bride
into the light
that at first was merely
a hesitating flicker
then burst
and splashed
a wondrous shadow.
We entered
and your hand did not leave mine
and you breathed my breath
and you were inside with me.
And although I knew that I'll return
to the dark, I glided into
the calm
of your
hand
holding
mine.

A SONG TO ORA

Again you're taking off into the sunlight
And I remain a cripple in a foreign world,
Where each repulsive scandal stuns me like a venom;
And lusty, greedy men cause my spirit to decay.

Each morning I hallucinate you gazing
Into a calm-blue of agitated land:
Where every tree and stone are forever praying
To a silent God that long forgot his covenant with them.

You're returning to a land of motherhood in mourning,
Where, with feverish hands, you beautify the earth;
While I stay here and rot among corrupted politicians
That plague this country with their foul breath.

But when my life is final, I shall return
To anemones and pines;
And you, delighted, welcome me
With white carnation and a book rhymes.

DAUGHTER OF MAN

Even if I hurt, I'll wipe the tears from my eyes
circumvent the obstacles of the sea,
skip the darkness of pits,
escape the venom of snakes, and leap into
the melting pastels.

I am cautious of man.
Even if he vows
you are the one. Forever.
I will yearn no more waiting in vain,
injured and dripping as if shot.
I will wrap my sorrow as a gift
and send it far beyond the sea,
the place of shadows and light
of my youth.

And even if my body collapses,
I'll free my spirit from steel
to a place where
the earth emits fragrance of life
the wind kisses daffodils' hearts
a baby shines primordial and pure.

I will flee from you and your deceitful ways

I, daughter of man.

A SONG FOR THE MUSE

How will I know if there's another song?
Each day I fear perhaps it is my last,
But must I be discouraged and forlorn,
Though be it true, yet never, never just.

Each morning I return to my page so stark
And fill it with the story of my turmoiled thought;
What are you, muse, if not a friend to souls that starve?
So do now what you do so well; sigh later if you must.

Don't disappoint or frown your lofty brow at me,
Remember, I am your friend steadfast,
Don't scold and glare with marble eyes at me,
Soften your mercurial heart and be a blast.

I'll sing for you my best of songs
I'll write my best of verse,
And you, my muse, will burst
With pride, and never shall digress.

A WINTER SONG

Again you will be absent in the winter
And every naked branch will scream your loss,
Every silver star will shun me till I wither,
Only pregnant clouds your name endorse.

With every passing day I'll glance with hesitation
At all those generous friends which tell us time;
And wipe a shameful tear with trembling trepidation
Praying to angry gods of nature to speed the budding-time.

Then, as an ancient lion, you'll stand before me,
Your aging torso bent, your mane a little thin,
But when it comes to you, believe me,
I'm mute and deaf, my eyes completely dim.

Blinded I will touch your face
With gentle palm
And watch you smile at me, like then,
When all with us was calm.

GIVE US A KISS

(A prose-poem-story)

For forty years, my heart leaped at the sound of *His* voice.
His name was a summon to my foolish blood.
Now my blood is old; slow and lazy, it courses through my
veins.
Forty years seems eternal, and yet when *He* calls
and asks me to meet him, I always say yes.
The force of habit clutches at my heart,
or perhaps, it is still a surge of love?
But that day (perhaps just to spite *Him*),
I don't say yes right away, I say that
I have to ask Teddy first.
"Really," *He* asks, surprised, "why?"
We both know that I don't have to ask Teddy.
He knows all about *Him* and me, and if he bears a grudge,
he keeps it to himself.
My darling Teddy, so worldly and bright, most understanding
and so gallant—

I wish
That you walk by my side
so I wouldn't have to travel again
this arduous way
alone.
That you'll protect me
so I wouldn't have to bleed
between rusty teeth
of concealed traps—
even from those who pretend
to be my friends.
That you never throw
unkind words at me,
only clasp my hand,
let the warmth of your touch
flow inside my heart
and fill me
with calm.

He calls again on Thursday and asks if I am free on Friday.
He must see me, *He* says it's urgent.
"I love you, doll," *He* says, his voice sonorous and sexy.
Oh, well, this I cannot ignore—What woman can?
So yes, I say, mimicking Molly Bloom's words,
"Yes, my love, yes, yes."
In the evening, when Teddy and I settle down
for light dinner of soup and bread
that Teddy made (I am a catastrophe
in the kitchen, Teddy is ace.)
I say, "Tomorrow I am going to dinner with *Him*."
Teddy's eyebrows rise. "With whom?" he asks.
"With *Him*," I bark, soup dripping from my mouth.

189

Teddy's lips pucker into a smile. "Oh, with *Him*."
Then he asks, "When will you be back?"
He pours himself another glass of wine, his fourth. (I count.)
"Never," I say then slide to the floor, feigning a faint.
(It is a sort of an absurd game between Teddy and me
when the atmosphere gets tight. And as infantile as my
antics are, it always makes him laugh.)
I yearn for Teddy to say, even once,
"That's enough, there is an end to everything,
you are my wife, and a wife should
be true to her husband, not run around."
But when Teddy asked me to be his wife,
he knew he made a package deal.
So, I give him a kiss and swear in my heart
to avenge myself on both of them one night
when the Milky Way is empty and stunned,
empty and stunned as was my heart,
deserted by *Him*, forty years ago, on that
sun-scorched beach to squirm and sizzle
in the malignant heat:

Sun stunned we met then on the beach, and
he looked at me shyly and asked, may I?
And I uttered, Of course, and felt my heart leaping
to my fingertips.
He smiled and sat close, not touching,
playing mindlessly with a conch.
Listen to the sea, he said,
pressing the conch to my ear.
I heard the sea simmering inside my brain:
Beware, beware.
But that same day
his body moved on mine,

and he cooed lustful words into my breasts,
under my naked body, sun-scorched, sand of noon,
shifting, twisting in a delirious swoon.
And he cooed lustful words into my breasts,
and I was burning, my brain inlaid with seashell shards,
and the sea shuddering, whispering, seething, growling
and the wind moaning mercilessly.
Then he tore his body from mine, standing up,
looking at me from somewhere far above,
and murmured shyly, "Thanks,"
and walked away.
I watched his distancing back
and saw waves of prey licking his feet,
and the sea swelling, frothing in a primal rage,
corpses of fishes floating on its waves,
and it roared in a terrible pain,
and the wind moaned mercilessly.

So when *He* calls on Friday, his voice fails
to stir me, and there is no spark in my soul, but
I say I'll meet him at the Ritz at seven for dinner.
What else can I do? Love of forty years
is impossible to smother just like that.
"I'll pick you up at your home," *He* says.
"Okay," I say (and scream at myself, and if I could,
I would have slapped my face)
because *He* wins again—he always does, and
yet, my heart remains cold.
Cold?
Then why the tingle in my toes,
and my pulse beats like an engine in my throat?
And then a hushed voice whispers
inside my head,

You say you love me,
you say you care.
Why then you play
rough with my feelings?
You expose your cruel streak,
your low self-esteem;
it simply isn't fair.
You say you're coming,
then come or don't say,
as it makes you a liar,
and it makes me your aim.

Friday.
At school, the teachers are agitated,
stressed from a most intense week
longing for home,—so are the children,
and of course, me too.
When I enter my house, I drop my purse
on the couch and march straight to the mirror.
"Mirror, mirror on the wall,
who is the dumbest of them all?"
My face stares back at me tight and glossy—
so what if I had a little help with stretching and all?
You're so narcissistic, whispers the hushed voice,

after all
No one has benefited
from your beauty
even a dog you didn't train
only yourself you pester
how do I look?
what is my image today?

"Go away, leave me be," I shriek and thrust my
fingers into my ears and begin to cry.

I don't change my clothes, nor take my makeup off.
I go to the huge window and sit in my big black chair,
smoke a cigarette, and gaze into the street.—How pretty.
Fall gazes back at me, benevolent but gloomy,
The soft maple trees stand bare and ghostly in the pallid air
and birds are only a vague memory of something
cheerful and soft.
I watch the evening shadows shroud the world
and try not to think pestering thoughts,
but the chatter in my brain won't cease,
buzzing like millions of wasps, memories of yesteryear,
when all was different
and the hushed voice whispers,

Remember?
There among the lemon trees and vineyards
through vivid sunrise and through dew
we didn't walk in vain,
our faces lifted to the sky,
basking in the Milky Way.
Of course, I remember. How can I forget?

But now, I wish to dwell
in the silence of the mind
to be shut inside a cask
from time to time,
carefully, peek outside
to breathe for a moment the light
to smile at a child,

and again dive into the
silence of my mind
and think
not see
expect nothing
only be,
for who am I, except
blood and tissues,
and hairs and veins,
and rotting cells . . .

But here the voice disappears
because suddenly, through my window,
I see a drunkard tottering in the street,
his face broken into a million pieces,
his hopes forgotten and dead.
He sits on the low cement by my gate
And with shaking hands, tries to light a cigarette.
But it's too windy, so he spits, he curses,
he takes a swig from his bottle and begins to stumble
but he steadies himself and doesn't tumble.
(Teddy cautions me repeatedly not to invite
"strangers" into the house. "It's too risky," he says,
"you might get yourself raped." He's aware of my weakness
for the unfortunate, the miserable, the homeless.
But this is a subject to be explored somewhere else.)
Teddy himself likes his wine strong and red.
Anyway, the drunk walks away and disappears
into the evening, carrying with him his shattered image.
A young woman with a poodle on a velvet leash
is trotting along the street, her eyes are dreamy
and there's a silly smile on her lips.
A young man wearing a turned-around baseball hat

meets her. They laugh, they kiss, the hat falls, the poodle
barks,
but they pay it no heed.
Standing under my window, their bodies are glued,
and they are licking each other lustily.
"Beware of the undertow," I want to scream,
love is not what it seems.
But they vanish into the fog
of delusion.
When Teddy comes home, deep evening
has gathered the city into its shadows,
the world calmed down. The soft maple trees
have become spirits.
"My one and only," Teddy says and devours me with kisses.
I bury my face in the soft nook of his neck and implore him
not to let me go out with *Him*,—to keep me at home
where I am safe and warm.
But Teddy is deaf to my supplications because,
Of course, I only say it inside my head.

So, You be my judges, doesn't it serve me right?

I have slush in my heart,—an old old wound
if you open my brain, you will see
bleeding lacerated and unhealed scars,
but also, the old fire that still burns in me—
for there isn't enough earth to extinguish it . . .

Seven o'clock:
I wait.
The doorbell rings.
I don't stir.
Teddy glances at me, amused. I shrug my shoulders.

Teddy gets up and opens the door and who do you think
is standing there with a smile as wide as a summer night
and eyes as wet as rain, if not my *old knight.*
He looks at Teddy and me and smiles at us quietly.
"Are you ready, doll?" *He* asks gently, then shakes
Teddy's hand and says, "Hi, Ted, how good to see you."
"Sit down," says Teddy. "Would you like a glass of wine?"
"No thanks," *He* answers, "perhaps some other time."
"Bye," says my Teddy, "enjoy the evening," and he pats my
head, as if I were his daughter, then gives me a hurried kiss.
My heart doesn't crumble, it moans, and as I walk to
the door, I trip on the rug (like the drunk, remember?)
and almost tumble.—Four arms reach out and hold me,
but my ears are ringing and I begin to snort. I kick the wall.
No one sees, no one knows, because, it isn't me,—
It's only my ghost. I shoot a murderous look at Teddy
but he merely smiles and pinches my cheek and I am
tempted to hit him, but immediately the hushed voice
is there to remind me that when I met Teddy:

He came in the dark
and took my hand
and led me, a bride,
into the light
that at first was merely
a hesitating flicker then burst
and splashed
a wondrous shadow.
We entered
and his hand did not leave mine
and he breathed my breath
and was inside with me.
And although I knew that I'll return

to the dark,
I glided into
the calm
of his
hand
holding
mine.

And so it is.
He and me again going into the night—,
so far away from that burning white beach
where we first met forty years ago.
He holds my hand and says for the
millionth and one time, "You're so pretty, doll."
But I am not as quick as all that, I am still thinking
of the drunkard, of Teddy, and of the love-stricken lady.
He kisses me, and they all fade except Teddy.
"I love you," *He* says, his voice, deep and steady—,
and suddenly my Teddy disappears too,
and my world turns crazy.

About the rest of that evening, the other voice will tell you.
Please listen!

The rest of that evening is peaches and cream
dimmed lights and pink champagne
poisoned with dreams,
and gray snails on a blood-red platter,
slippery and slimy as the gutter.
Murmurs wafting in the smoke-filled air
and memories of love lurking everywhere,
and shadow-like touches
and words filled with lies and ashes.

Hollow shadows grinning wide
like jackals on a starlit night.
Time is bewitched
I am glowing, I am flying, but
between us a wall of fog is lying,
and I am hateful and my body tears.
Flutter of lips in the dark like the flutter of moths' wings
and from a black man, like lava from a dark mountain,
irrupts love songs that
even God has forgotten.
Suddenly
a scorching heat, a whisper,
"Are you with me, my love?"
And I know,
again
the time has
come to part,
and a stony silence
fills my heart.

Freaky huh?

And then, at ten, on the porch of my home,
He kisses my lips in a beastly heat,
and abandons me as he always did.
(His wife is waiting.)
I sit on the steps; bury my face in my hands,
and slowly return to myself.
As I open the door, I see Teddy still staring at the television
as if enchanted because, naturally, he takes the whole
thing completely for granted.
"Hello, my love," he says, "did you enjoy yourself?"
He isn't joking, but I detect a slight tension in his eyes.

"I drank a lot of champagne and had a ball."
Teddy laughs, his face relaxes. "Give us a kiss, my love, eh,"
he says and slaps his knee. And I go to him and sit
in his lap and wrap my arms around his neck while *his* gentle
voice is still vibrating in my brain, and the champagne is still
buzzing confusion in my head.
"But do you love me?" asks Teddy as he kisses my eyes.
Enough! I've had it for today!
So, I run to my room,
grab the old, reliable bong
out from its secret place,
and inhale grass
until I am good and stoned.
Then I shed my clothes,
murmur a curse
and, like a worm, squirm
into my bed
and cover my head,
thinking, *what a mess,*
I must stop this
or else.
But
what a waste
because
I love them
both
and know
that
I'll never
let go.

ILANA HALEY

HE AND SHE

And he is taut as pain
and she like water shimmers
and summer tongue is licking
a molten-crimson sky,
and wind-in-heat is twirling
coupling with gardens
and people come
and people go.
And he like heart is beating
and she like whore is teasing
and the river storms
the fish are going wild,
and a city-of-steel indulges
in blasts of fire-works.
And he is sharp as sorrow
and she is a flower weaving,
and shadows float
and shadows dive,
and eternity has no gates
only a breathless silence
and he her breasts is kissing
with violence of
war.

(And in that Garden the Serpent laughs)

CITY SPRING

Yesterday, Sunday,
I walked out my front door
And Spring came and sat next to me
On my front porch.
He was not Spring of my youth.
He did not smell of blossoms and first fruit.
He did not glow and glitter under a cloudless sky.
The air he brought with him was not transparent, not clean.
Birds did not follow him to nest in my soft maple tree.
He put his dusty head on my lap and sighed sadly.
He smelled of dry concrete and acid steel.
His eyes were glassy reflecting the cold marble of the city.
His voice, like a boom box, sounded shrill and brassy.
Pieces of dog shit stuck to his feet.
He apologized about his bad smell, untidy
Appearance, and unpleasant voice—
He asked my forgiveness for being ugly.
And of course, I would have preferred
To sit with him under an olive tree, look at
A bright azure sky, smell the fragrance of fields,
Or walk with him hand in hand on the beach, dipping
My sore toes in warm sand, smelling the salt-spiced air,
And watch with him the sunset over the sea—
Or perhaps merely look for—shells,
But I didn't tell him all that.
He was so pathetic; I didn't want to hurt him.
I patted his head and told him not to worry.
He is Spring, and he is welcome—smelly or fragrant,

Dirty or pure, as long as he is Spring.
He wrapped himself around me
In a hazy stench of car fumes and blasting noises
And kept me company for the rest of the day.
I sat with him for a long time
Reading a book and glancing from time to time
At the tiny buds that appeared overnight
On the soft maple tree.
I prayed for one bird to appear.
Give me a sign. Welcome, Spring.
A bird did not appear, but the neighbor's dog
Came and crapped on my front yard
Then smirked at me and trotted away.
I thought Spring would die from shame.
Well, maybe
Another
day.